ILLUSTRATION BY SHU YAN

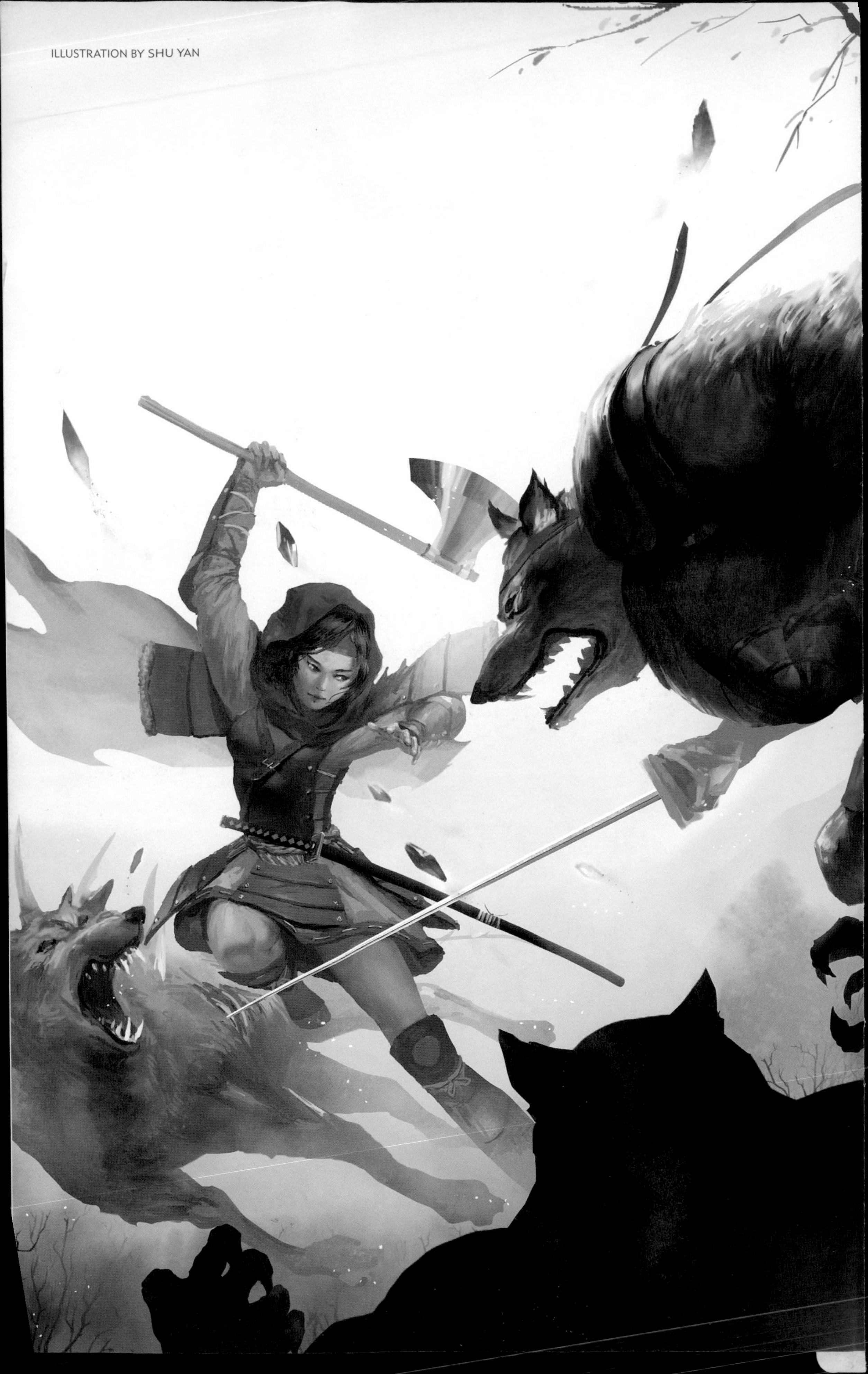

AKANEIRO™
The Path of Cloak and Wolf

STORY **JUSTIN ACLIN**

ART **VASILIS LOLOS**

COLORS **MICHAEL ATIYEH**

LETTERING **MICHAEL HEISLER**

FRONT COVER ART **SHU YAN**

DARK HORSE BOOKS

PUBLISHER MIKE RICHARDSON

DESIGNER ADAM GRANO

ASSISTANT EDITOR IAN TUCKER

EDITOR DAVE MARSHALL

Special thanks to Spicy Horse Games, including American McGee, R. J. Berg, and Benjamin Kerslake.

AKANEIRO: THE PATH OF CLOAK AND WOLF

This volume collects issues one through three of the Dark Horse comic-book miniseries *Akaneiro*.

Published by
Dark Horse Books
A division of
Dark Horse Comics, Inc.
10956 SE Main Street
Milwaukie, OR 97222

DarkHorse.com
SpicyHorse.com

Aclin, Justin, author.
Akaneiro : the Path of Cloak and Wolf / story, Justin Aclin ; art, Vasilis Lolos ; colors, Michael Atiyeh ; lettering, Michael Heisler ; front cover art, Shu Yan. — First edition.
pages cm
ISBN 978-1-61655-194-0
1. Graphic novels. I. Lolos, Vasilis, illustrator. II. Title.
PN6727.A266A38 2013
741.5'973—dc23
2013026264

First edition: November 2013
10 9 8 7 6 5 4 3 2 1
Printed in China

Mike Richardson, President and Publisher | Neil Hankerson, Executive Vice President | Tom Weddle, Chief Financial Officer | Randy Stradley, Vice President of Publishing | Michael Martens, Vice President of Book Trade Sales | Anita Nelson, Vice President of Business Affairs | Scott Allie, Editor in Chief | Matt Parkinson, Vice President of Marketing | David Scroggy, Vice President of Product Development | Dale LaFountain, Vice President of Information Technology | Darlene Vogel, Senior Director of Print, Design, and Production | Ken Lizzi, General Counsel | Davey Estrada, Editorial Director | Chris Warner, Senior Books Editor | Diana Schutz, Executive Editor | Cary Grazzini, Director of Print and Development | Lia Ribacchi, Art Director | Cara Niece, Director of Scheduling | Tim Wiesch, Director of International Licensing | Mark Bernardi, Director of Digital Publishing

ILLUSTRATION BY SHU YAN

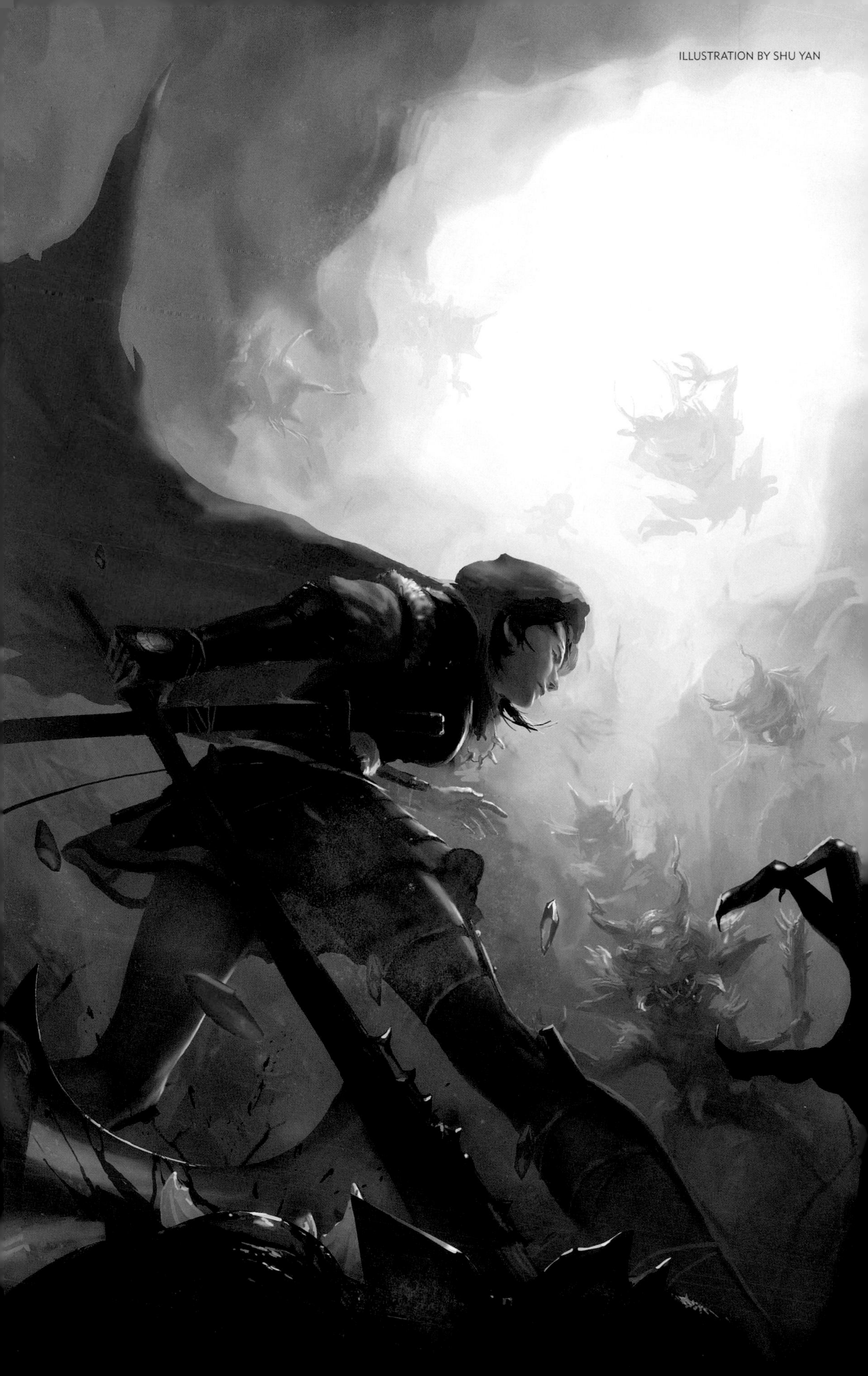

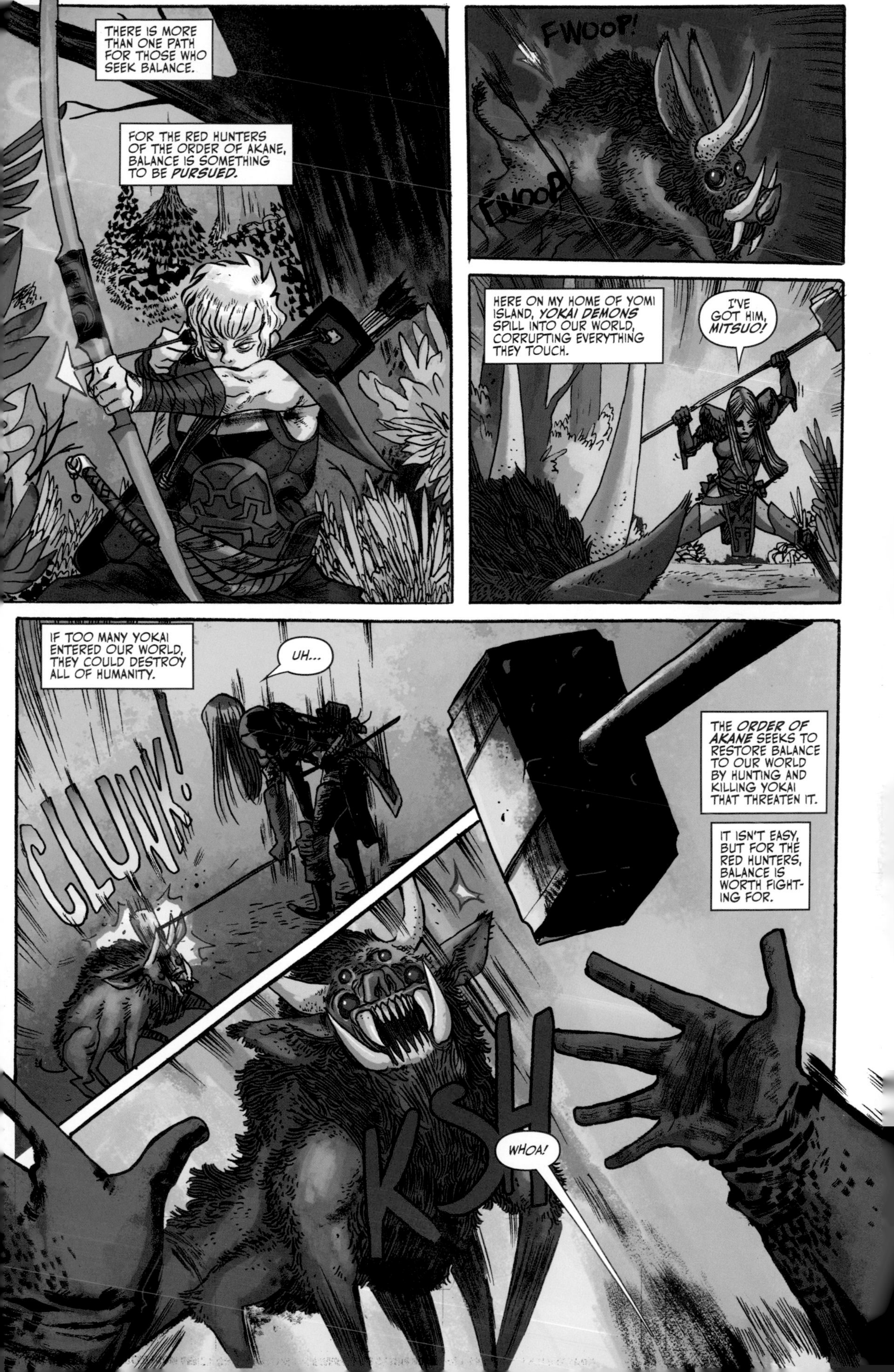
THERE IS MORE THAN ONE PATH FOR THOSE WHO SEEK BALANCE.
FOR THE RED HUNTERS OF THE ORDER OF AKANE, BALANCE IS SOMETHING TO BE *PURSUED.*
FWOOP!
FWOOP!
HERE ON MY HOME OF YOMI ISLAND, *YOKAI DEMONS* SPILL INTO OUR WORLD, CORRUPTING EVERYTHING THEY TOUCH.
I'VE GOT HIM, *MITSUO!*
IF TOO MANY YOKAI ENTERED OUR WORLD, THEY COULD DESTROY ALL OF HUMANITY.
UH...
CLUNK!
THE *ORDER OF AKANE* SEEKS TO RESTORE BALANCE TO OUR WORLD BY HUNTING AND KILLING YOKAI THAT THREATEN IT.
IT ISN'T EASY, BUT FOR THE RED HUNTERS, BALANCE IS WORTH FIGHTING FOR.
KSH
WHOA!

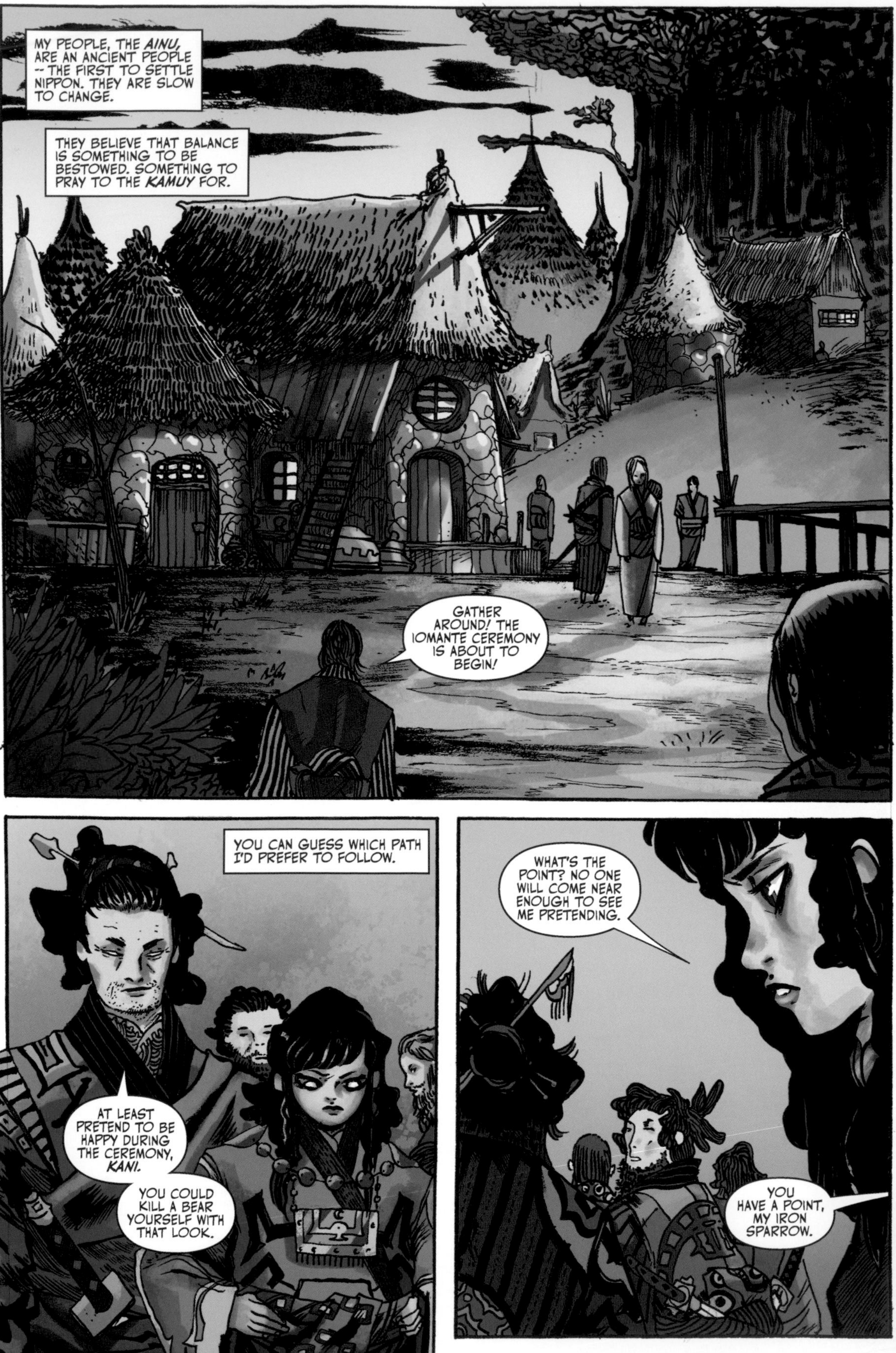
MY PEOPLE, THE AINU, ARE AN ANCIENT PEOPLE -- THE FIRST TO SETTLE NIPPON. THEY ARE SLOW TO CHANGE.
THEY BELIEVE THAT BALANCE IS SOMETHING TO BE BESTOWED. SOMETHING TO PRAY TO THE KAMUY FOR.
GATHER AROUND! THE IOMANTE CEREMONY IS ABOUT TO BEGIN!
YOU CAN GUESS WHICH PATH I'D PREFER TO FOLLOW.
AT LEAST PRETEND TO BE HAPPY DURING THE CEREMONY, KANI.
YOU COULD KILL A BEAR YOURSELF WITH THAT LOOK.
WHAT'S THE POINT? NO ONE WILL COME NEAR ENOUGH TO SEE ME PRETENDING.
YOU HAVE A POINT, MY IRON SPARROW.

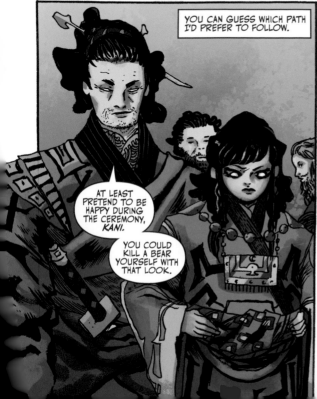

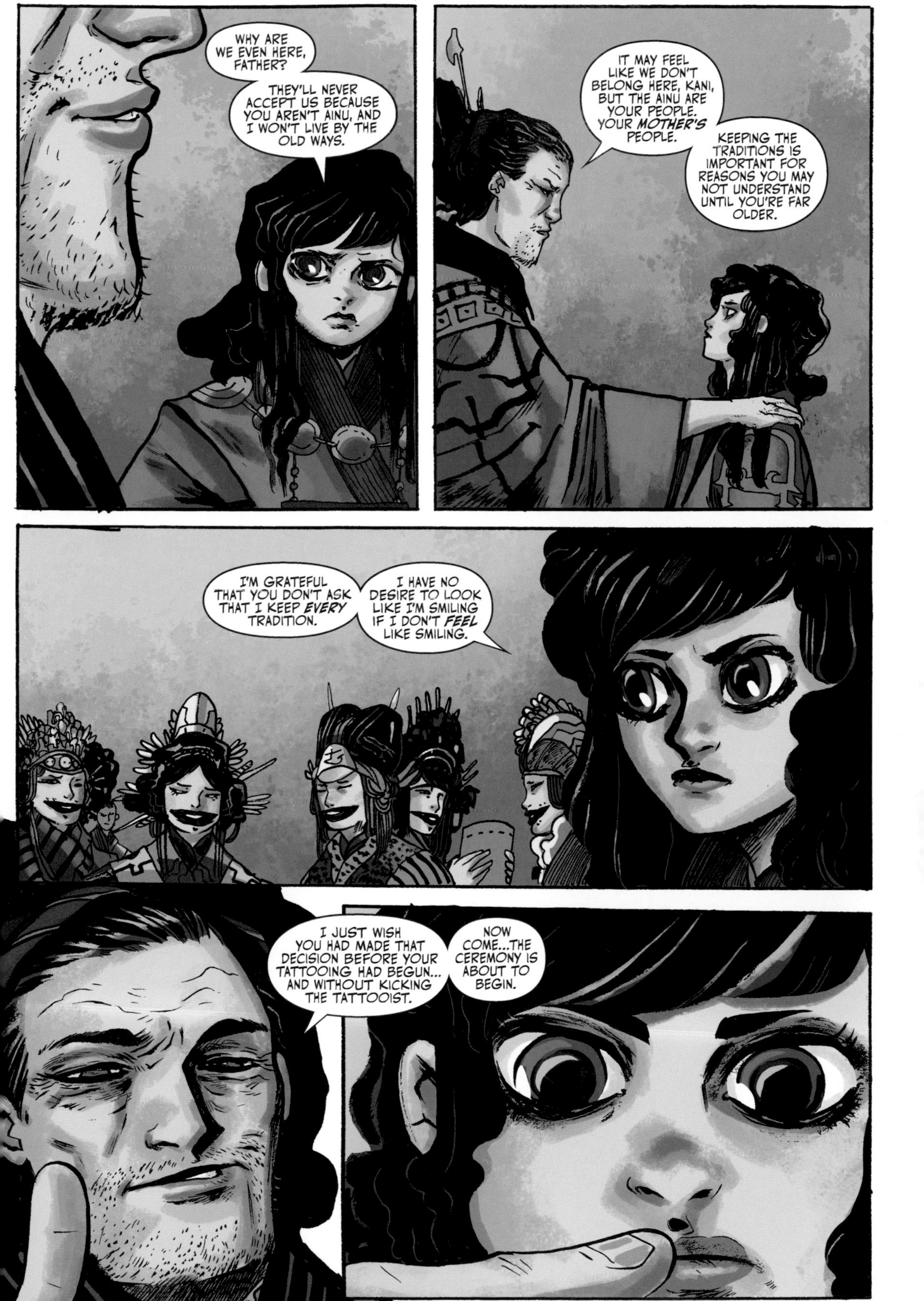
WHY ARE WE EVEN HERE, FATHER?
THEY'LL NEVER ACCEPT US BECAUSE YOU AREN'T AINU, AND I WON'T LIVE BY THE OLD WAYS.
IT MAY FEEL LIKE WE DON'T BELONG HERE, KANI, BUT THE AINU ARE YOUR PEOPLE. YOUR MOTHER'S PEOPLE.
KEEPING THE TRADITIONS IS IMPORTANT FOR REASONS YOU MAY NOT UNDERSTAND UNTIL YOU'RE FAR OLDER.
I'M GRATEFUL THAT YOU DON'T ASK THAT I KEEP EVERY TRADITION.
I HAVE NO DESIRE TO LOOK LIKE I'M SMILING IF I DON'T FEEL LIKE SMILING.
I JUST WISH YOU HAD MADE THAT DECISION BEFORE YOUR TATTOOING HAD BEGUN... AND WITHOUT KICKING THE TATTOOIST.
NOW COME...THE CEREMONY IS ABOUT TO BEGIN.

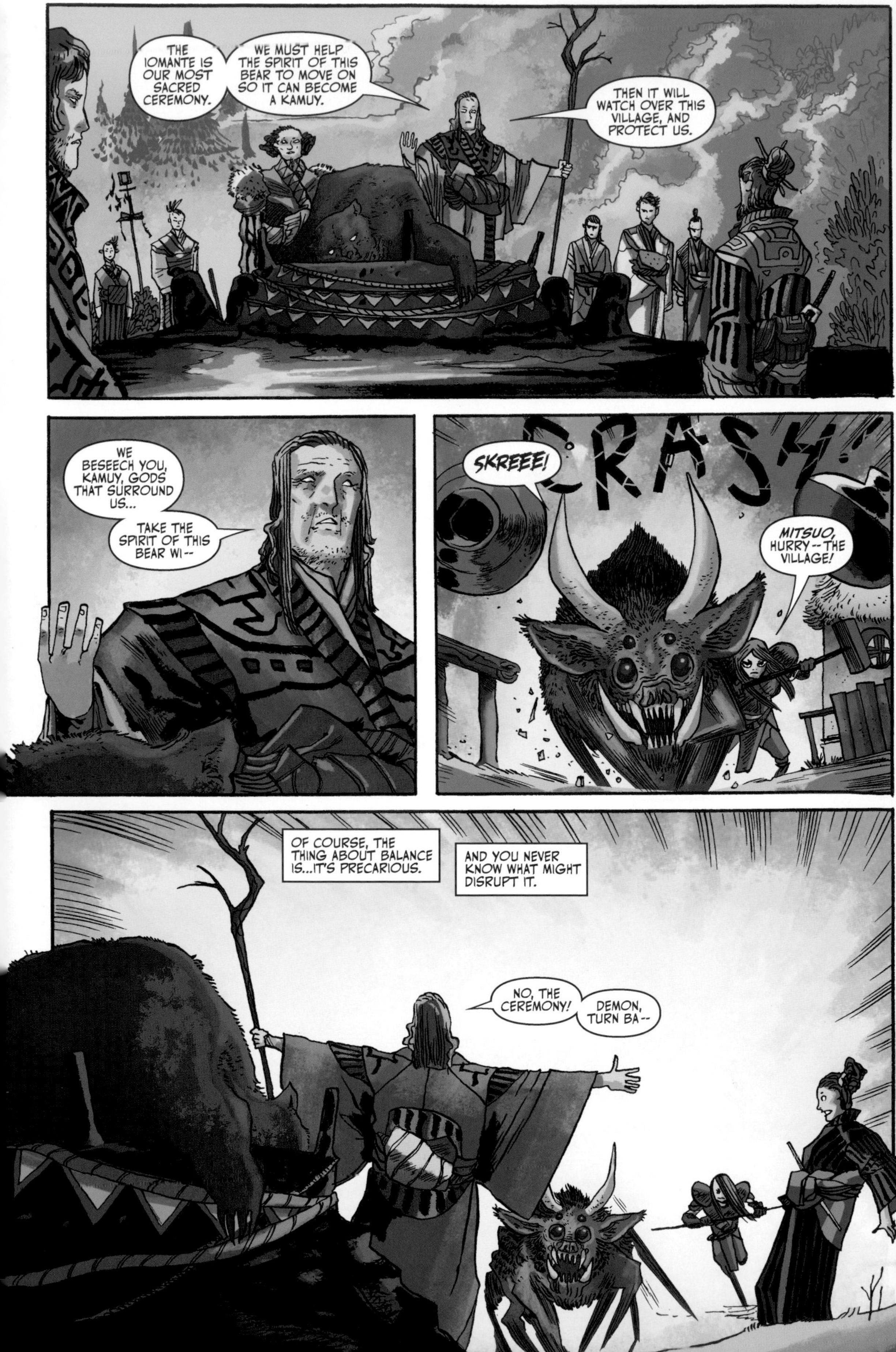
THE IOMANTE IS OUR MOST SACRED CEREMONY.
WE MUST HELP THE SPIRIT OF THIS BEAR TO MOVE ON SO IT CAN BECOME A KAMUY.
THEN IT WILL WATCH OVER THIS VILLAGE, AND PROTECT US.
WE BESEECH YOU, KAMUY, GODS THAT SURROUND US...
TAKE THE SPIRIT OF THIS BEAR WI--
CRASH!
SKREEE!
MITSUO, HURRY--THE VILLAGE!
OF COURSE, THE THING ABOUT BALANCE IS...IT'S PRECARIOUS.
AND YOU NEVER KNOW WHAT MIGHT DISRUPT IT.
NO, THE CEREMONY!
DEMON, TURN BA--

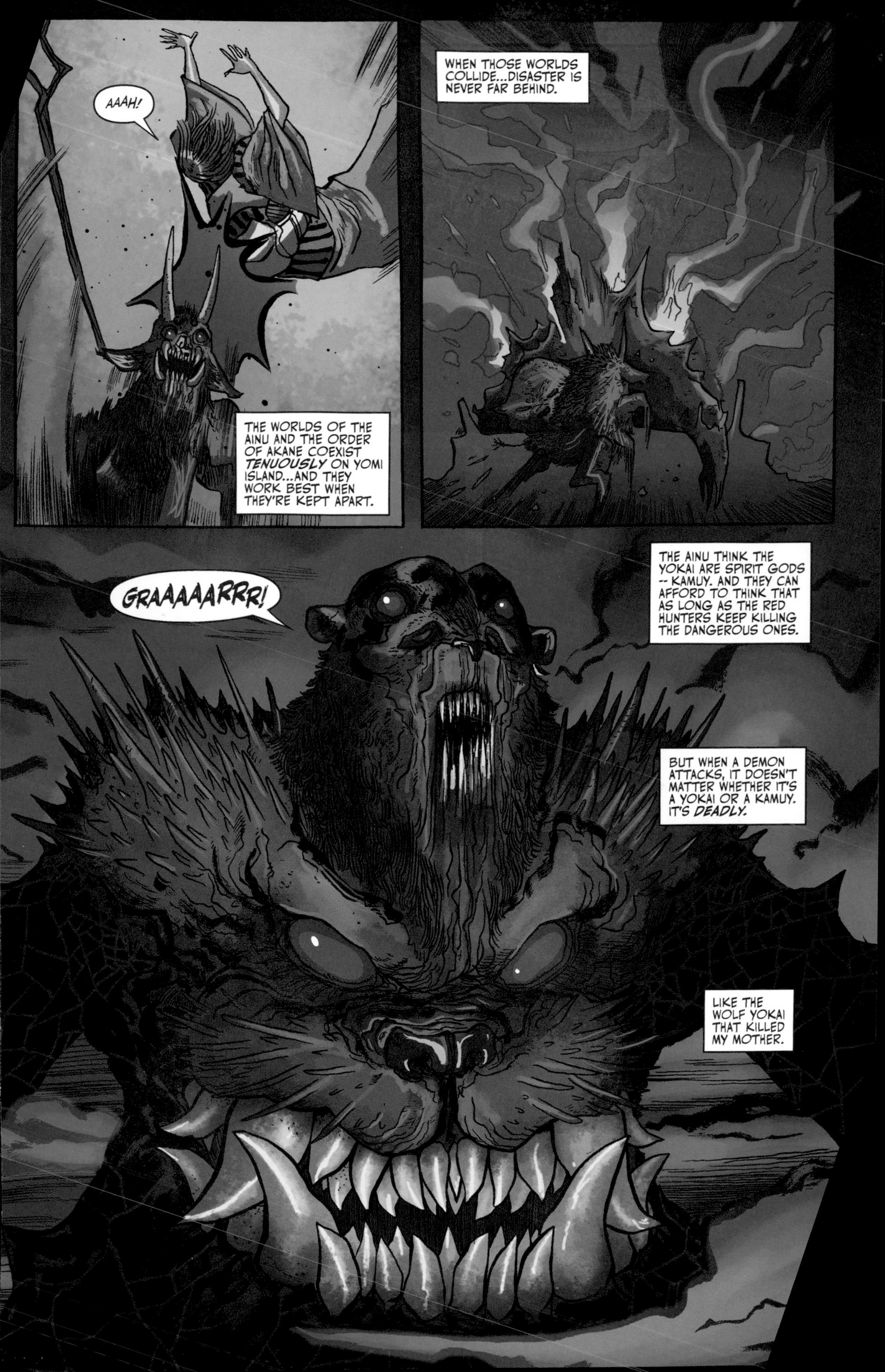
AAAH!
THE WORLDS OF THE AINU AND THE ORDER OF AKANE COEXIST TENUOUSLY ON YOMI ISLAND...AND THEY WORK BEST WHEN THEY'RE KEPT APART.
WHEN THOSE WORLDS COLLIDE...DISASTER IS NEVER FAR BEHIND.
GRAAAAARRR!
THE AINU THINK THE YOKAI ARE SPIRIT GODS -- KAMUY. AND THEY CAN AFFORD TO THINK THAT AS LONG AS THE RED HUNTERS KEEP KILLING THE DANGEROUS ONES.
BUT WHEN A DEMON ATTACKS, IT DOESN'T MATTER WHETHER IT'S A YOKAI OR A KAMUY. IT'S DEADLY.
LIKE THE WOLF YOKAI THAT KILLED MY MOTHER.

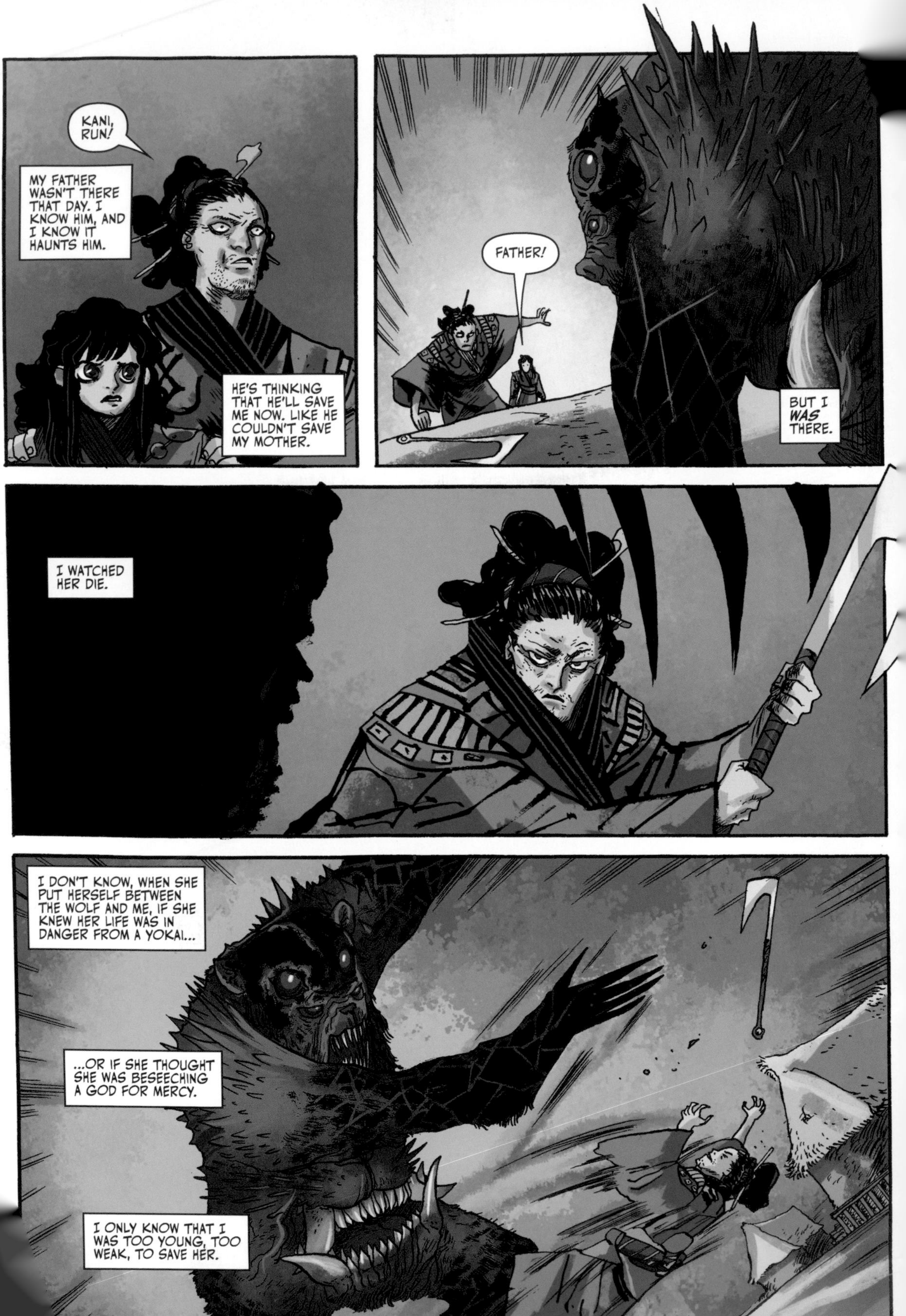
KANI, RUN!
MY FATHER WASN'T THERE THAT DAY. I KNOW HIM, AND I KNOW IT HAUNTS HIM.
HE'S THINKING THAT HE'LL SAVE ME NOW. LIKE HE COULDN'T SAVE MY MOTHER.
FATHER!
BUT I WAS THERE.
I WATCHED HER DIE.
I DON'T KNOW, WHEN SHE PUT HERSELF BETWEEN THE WOLF AND ME, IF SHE KNEW HER LIFE WAS IN DANGER FROM A YOKAI...
...OR IF SHE THOUGHT SHE WAS BESEECHING A GOD FOR MERCY.
I ONLY KNOW THAT I WAS TOO YOUNG, TOO WEAK, TO SAVE HER.

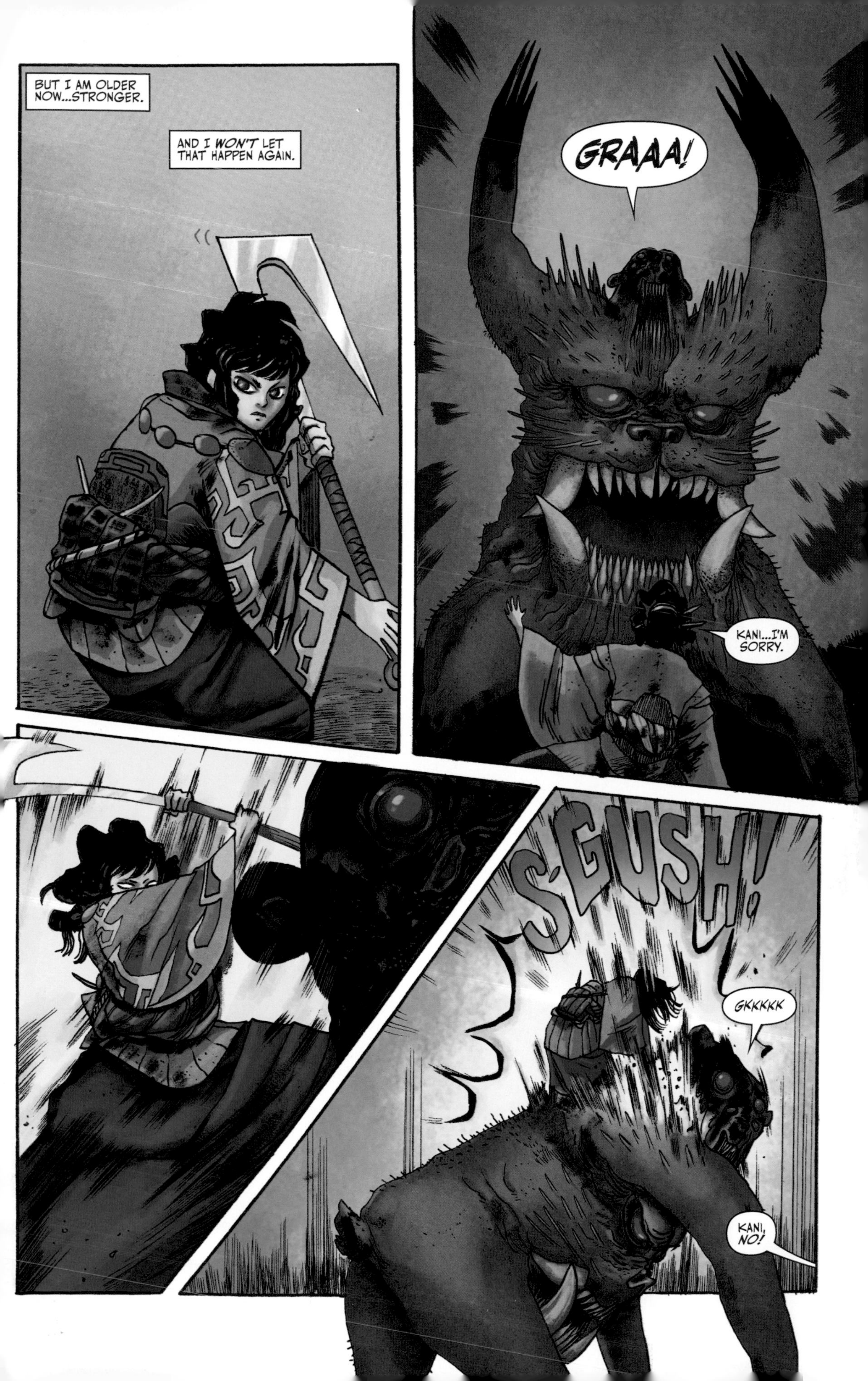
BUT I AM OLDER NOW...STRONGER.
AND I *WON'T* LET THAT HAPPEN AGAIN.
GRAAA!
KANI...I'M SORRY.
S'GUSH!
GKKKKK
KANI, *NO!*

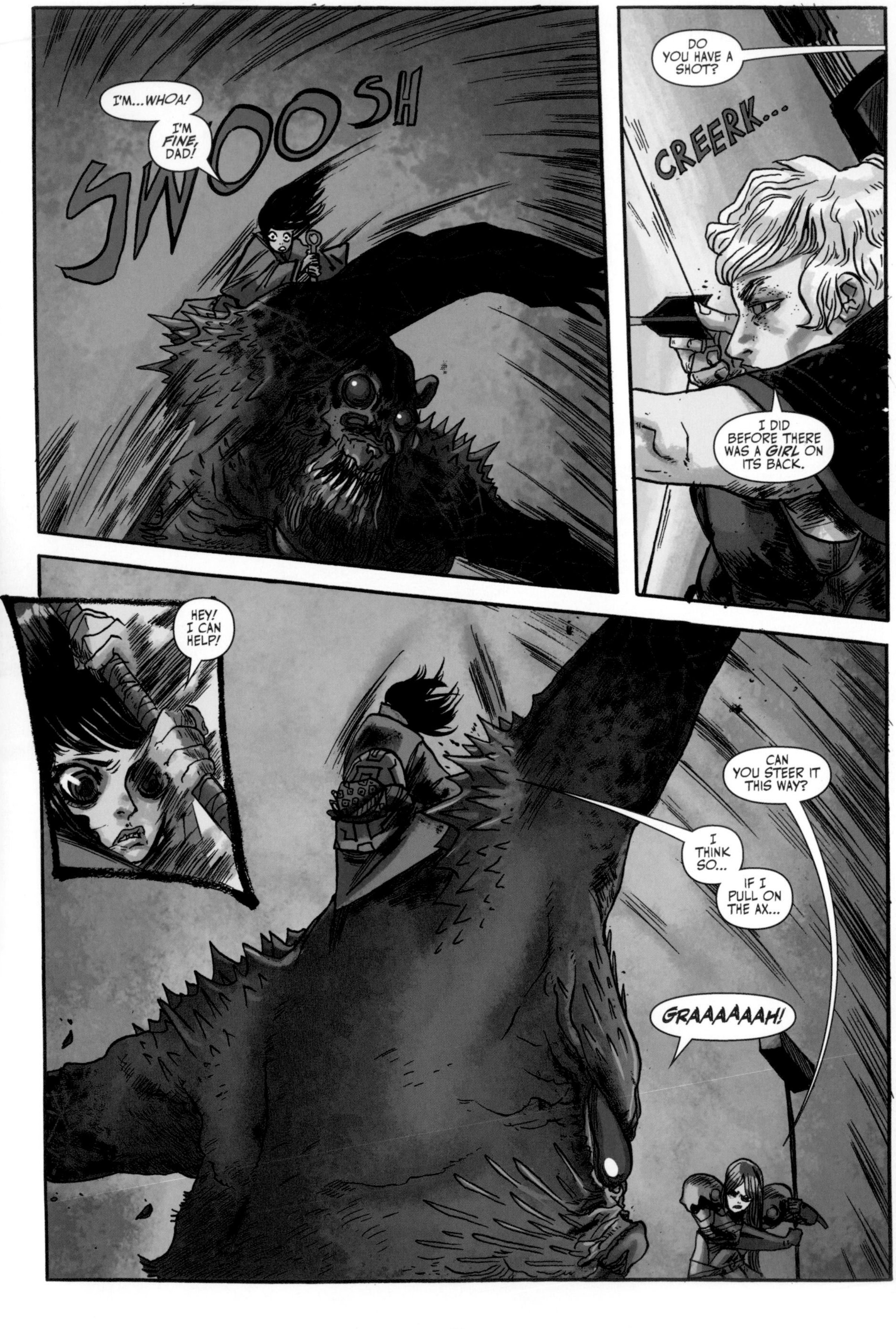
I'M...WHOA!
I'M FINE, DAD!
SWOOOSH
DO YOU HAVE A SHOT?
CREERK...
I DID BEFORE THERE WAS A GIRL ON ITS BACK.
HEY! I CAN HELP!
CAN YOU STEER IT THIS WAY?
I THINK SO...
IF I PULL ON THE AX...
GRAAAAAAH!

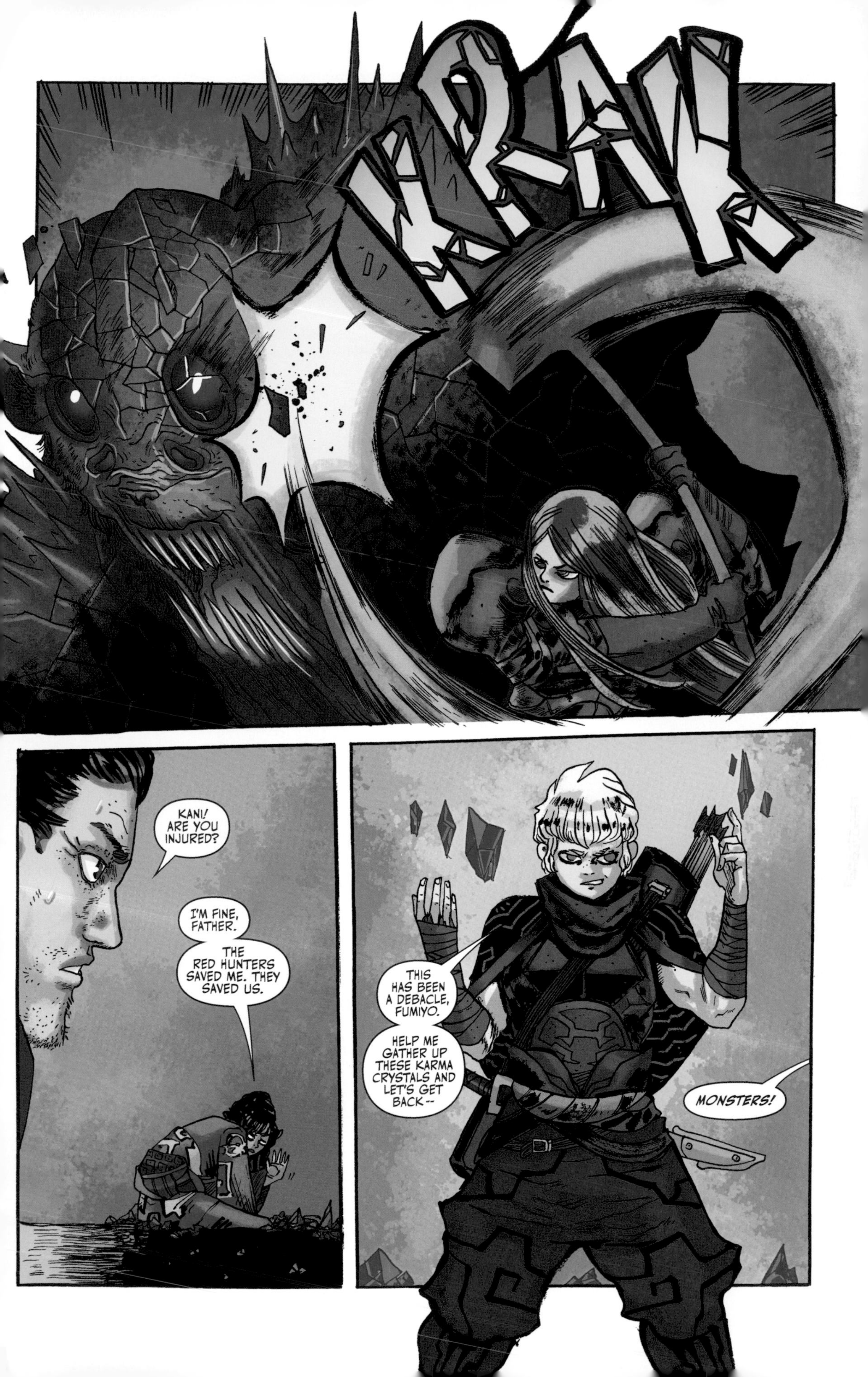
KRAK
KANI! ARE YOU INJURED?
I'M FINE, FATHER.
THE RED HUNTERS SAVED ME. THEY SAVED US.
THIS HAS BEEN A DEBACLE, FUMIYO.
HELP ME GATHER UP THESE KARMA CRYSTALS AND LET'S GET BACK--
MONSTERS!

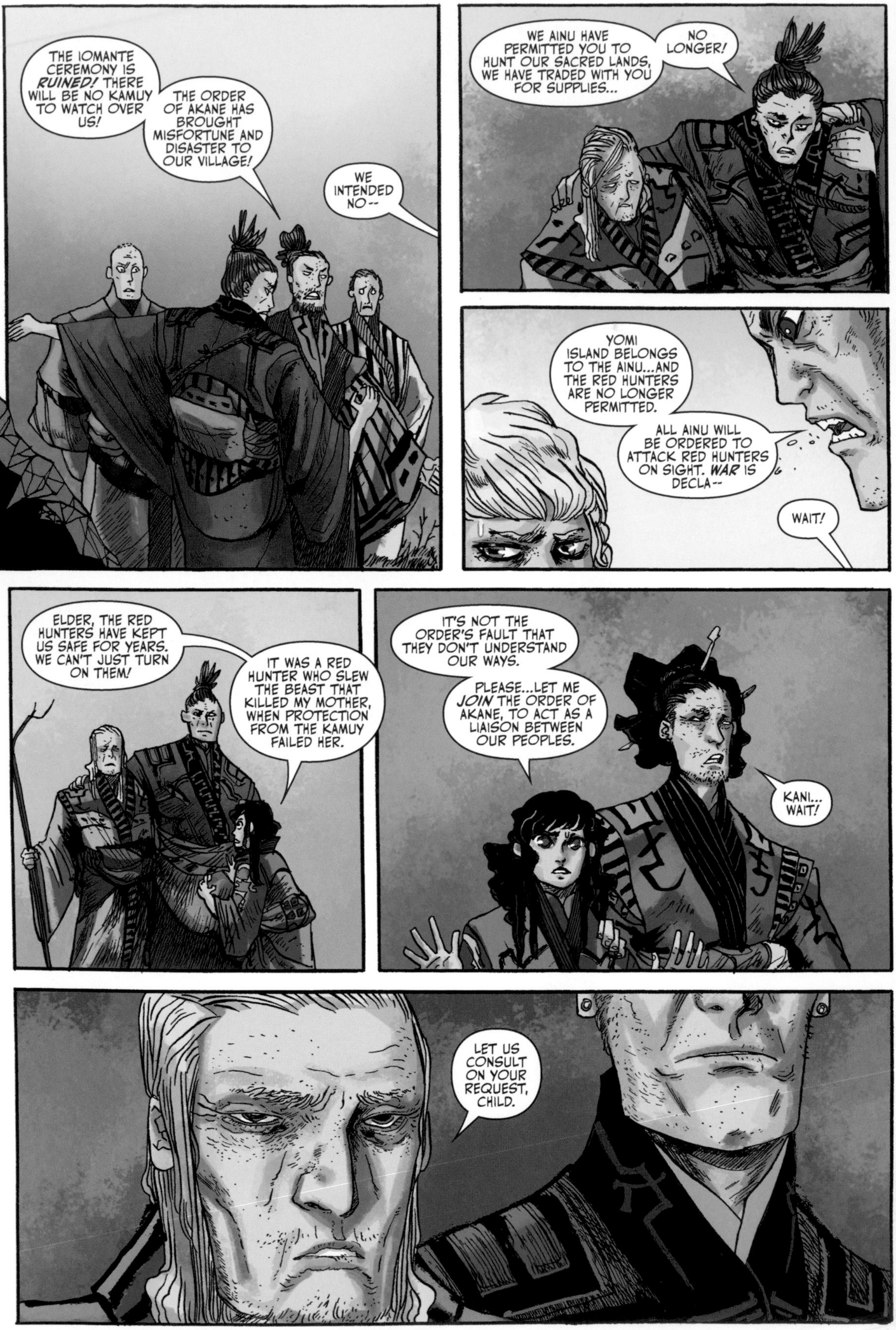
THE IOMANTE CEREMONY IS RUINED! THERE WILL BE NO KAMUY TO WATCH OVER US!
THE ORDER OF AKANE HAS BROUGHT MISFORTUNE AND DISASTER TO OUR VILLAGE!
WE INTENDED NO--
WE AINU HAVE PERMITTED YOU TO HUNT OUR SACRED LANDS, WE HAVE TRADED WITH YOU FOR SUPPLIES...
NO LONGER!
YOMI ISLAND BELONGS TO THE AINU...AND THE RED HUNTERS ARE NO LONGER PERMITTED.
ALL AINU WILL BE ORDERED TO ATTACK RED HUNTERS ON SIGHT. WAR IS DECLA--
WAIT!
ELDER, THE RED HUNTERS HAVE KEPT US SAFE FOR YEARS. WE CAN'T JUST TURN ON THEM!
IT WAS A RED HUNTER WHO SLEW THE BEAST THAT KILLED MY MOTHER, WHEN PROTECTION FROM THE KAMUY FAILED HER.
IT'S NOT THE ORDER'S FAULT THAT THEY DON'T UNDERSTAND OUR WAYS.
PLEASE...LET ME JOIN THE ORDER OF AKANE, TO ACT AS A LIAISON BETWEEN OUR PEOPLES.
KANI... WAIT!
LET US CONSULT ON YOUR REQUEST, CHILD.

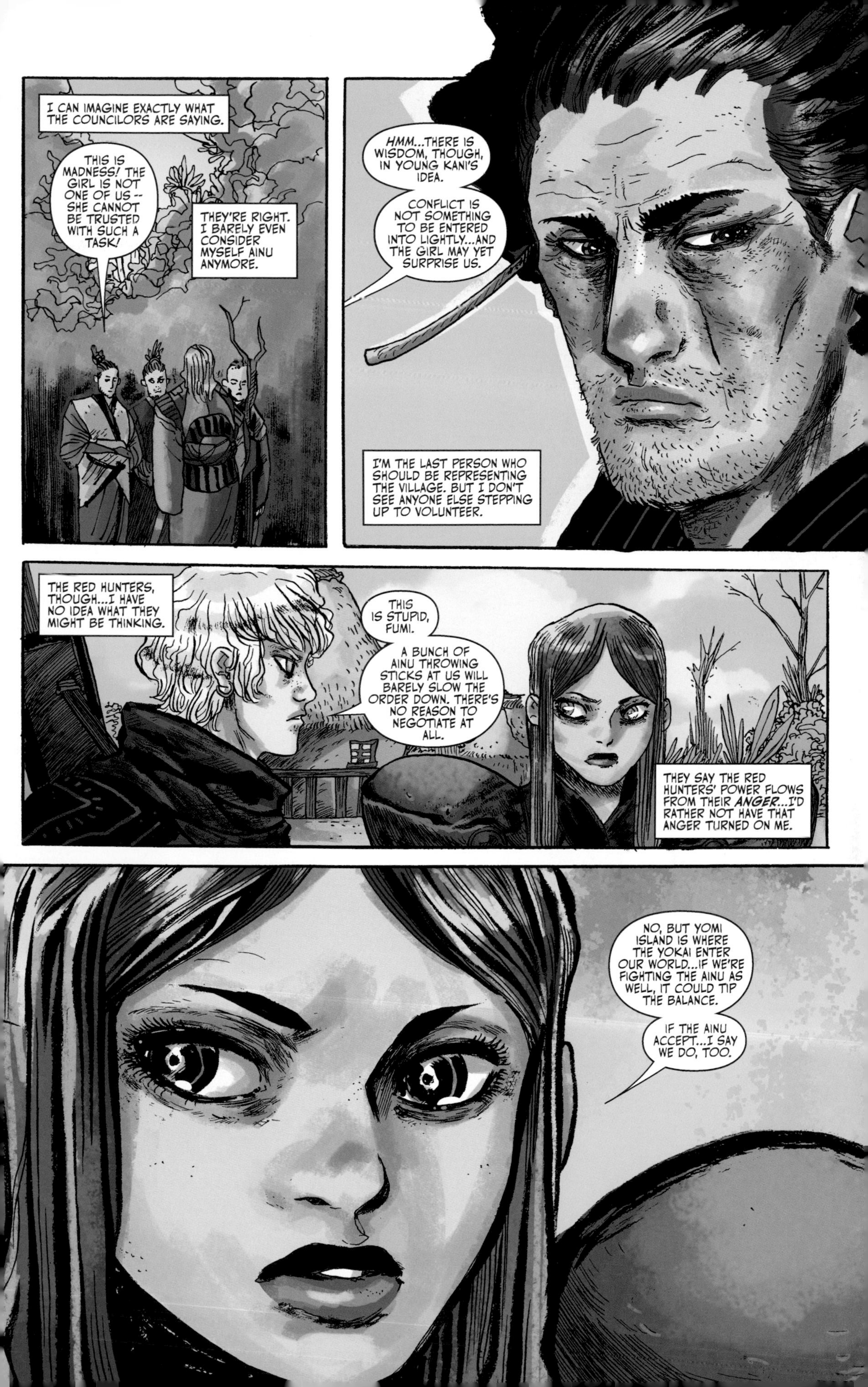
I CAN IMAGINE EXACTLY WHAT THE COUNCILORS ARE SAYING.
THIS IS MADNESS! THE GIRL IS NOT ONE OF US -- SHE CANNOT BE TRUSTED WITH SUCH A TASK!
THEY'RE RIGHT. I BARELY EVEN CONSIDER MYSELF AINU ANYMORE.
HMM...THERE IS WISDOM, THOUGH, IN YOUNG KANI'S IDEA.
CONFLICT IS NOT SOMETHING TO BE ENTERED INTO LIGHTLY...AND THE GIRL MAY YET SURPRISE US.
I'M THE LAST PERSON WHO SHOULD BE REPRESENTING THE VILLAGE. BUT I DON'T SEE ANYONE ELSE STEPPING UP TO VOLUNTEER.
THE RED HUNTERS, THOUGH...I HAVE NO IDEA WHAT THEY MIGHT BE THINKING.
THIS IS STUPID, FUMI.
A BUNCH OF AINU THROWING STICKS AT US WILL BARELY SLOW THE ORDER DOWN. THERE'S NO REASON TO NEGOTIATE AT ALL.
THEY SAY THE RED HUNTERS' POWER FLOWS FROM THEIR ANGER...I'D RATHER NOT HAVE THAT ANGER TURNED ON ME.
NO, BUT YOMI ISLAND IS WHERE THE YOKAI ENTER OUR WORLD...IF WE'RE FIGHTING THE AINU AS WELL, IT COULD TIP THE BALANCE.
IF THE AINU ACCEPT...I SAY WE DO, TOO.

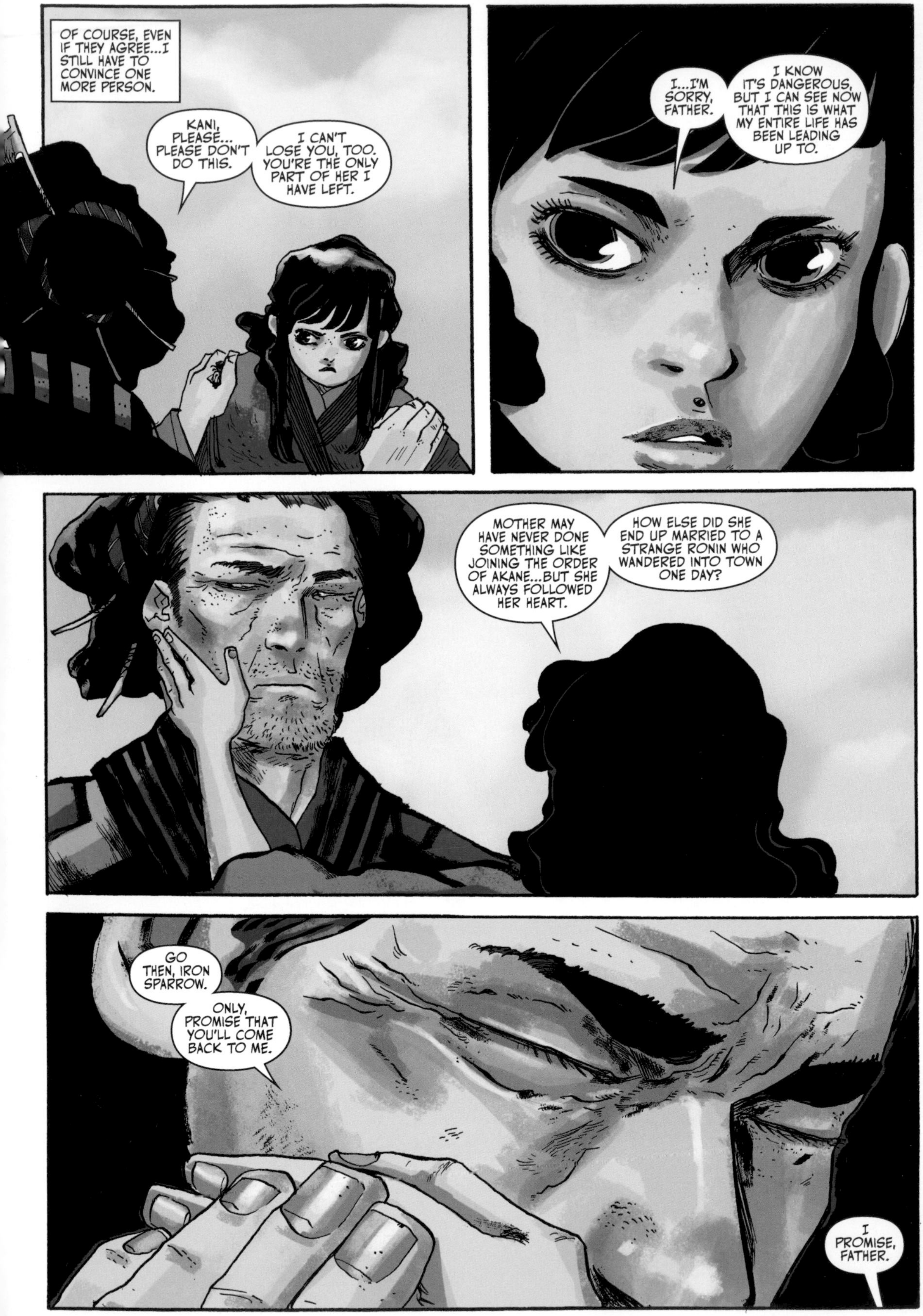

OF COURSE, EVEN IF THEY AGREE...I STILL HAVE TO CONVINCE ONE MORE PERSON.
KANI, PLEASE... PLEASE DON'T DO THIS.
I CAN'T LOSE YOU, TOO. YOU'RE THE ONLY PART OF HER I HAVE LEFT.
I...I'M SORRY, FATHER.
I KNOW IT'S DANGEROUS, BUT I CAN SEE NOW THAT THIS IS WHAT MY ENTIRE LIFE HAS BEEN LEADING UP TO.
MOTHER MAY HAVE NEVER DONE SOMETHING LIKE JOINING THE ORDER OF AKANE...BUT SHE ALWAYS FOLLOWED HER HEART.
HOW ELSE DID SHE END UP MARRIED TO A STRANGE RONIN WHO WANDERED INTO TOWN ONE DAY?
GO THEN, IRON SPARROW.
ONLY, PROMISE THAT YOU'LL COME BACK TO ME.
I PROMISE, FATHER.

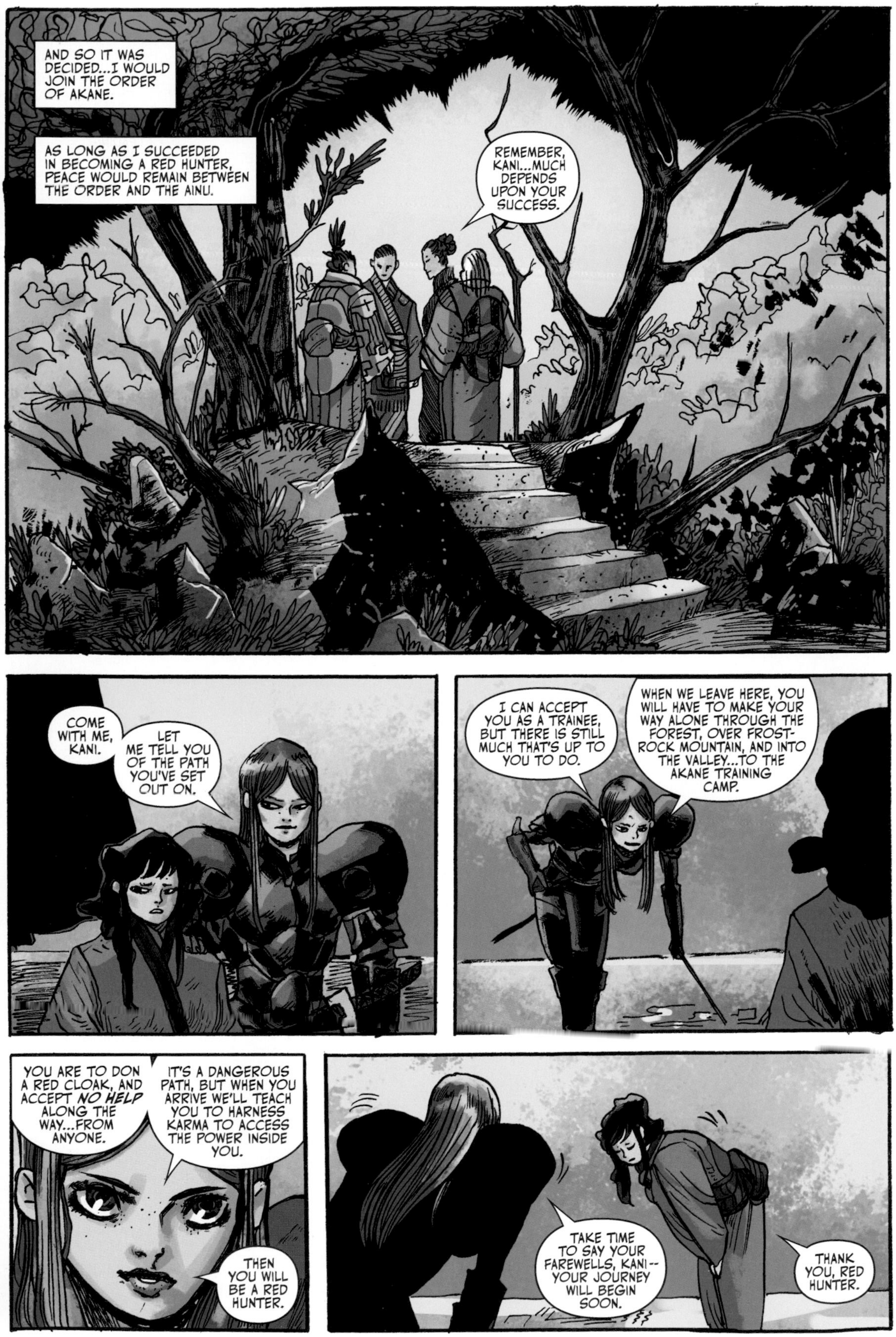
AND SO IT WAS DECIDED...I WOULD JOIN THE ORDER OF AKANE.
AS LONG AS I SUCCEEDED IN BECOMING A RED HUNTER, PEACE WOULD REMAIN BETWEEN THE ORDER AND THE AINU.
REMEMBER, KANI...MUCH DEPENDS UPON YOUR SUCCESS.
COME WITH ME, KANI.
LET ME TELL YOU OF THE PATH YOU'VE SET OUT ON.
I CAN ACCEPT YOU AS A TRAINEE, BUT THERE IS STILL MUCH THAT'S UP TO YOU TO DO.
WHEN WE LEAVE HERE, YOU WILL HAVE TO MAKE YOUR WAY ALONE THROUGH THE FOREST, OVER FROST-ROCK MOUNTAIN, AND INTO THE VALLEY...TO THE AKANE TRAINING CAMP.
YOU ARE TO DON A RED CLOAK, AND ACCEPT ***NO HELP*** ALONG THE WAY...FROM ANYONE.
IT'S A DANGEROUS PATH, BUT WHEN YOU ARRIVE WE'LL TEACH YOU TO HARNESS KARMA TO ACCESS THE POWER INSIDE YOU.
THEN YOU WILL BE A RED HUNTER.
TAKE TIME TO SAY YOUR FAREWELLS, KANI-- YOUR JOURNEY WILL BEGIN SOON.
THANK YOU, RED HUNTER.

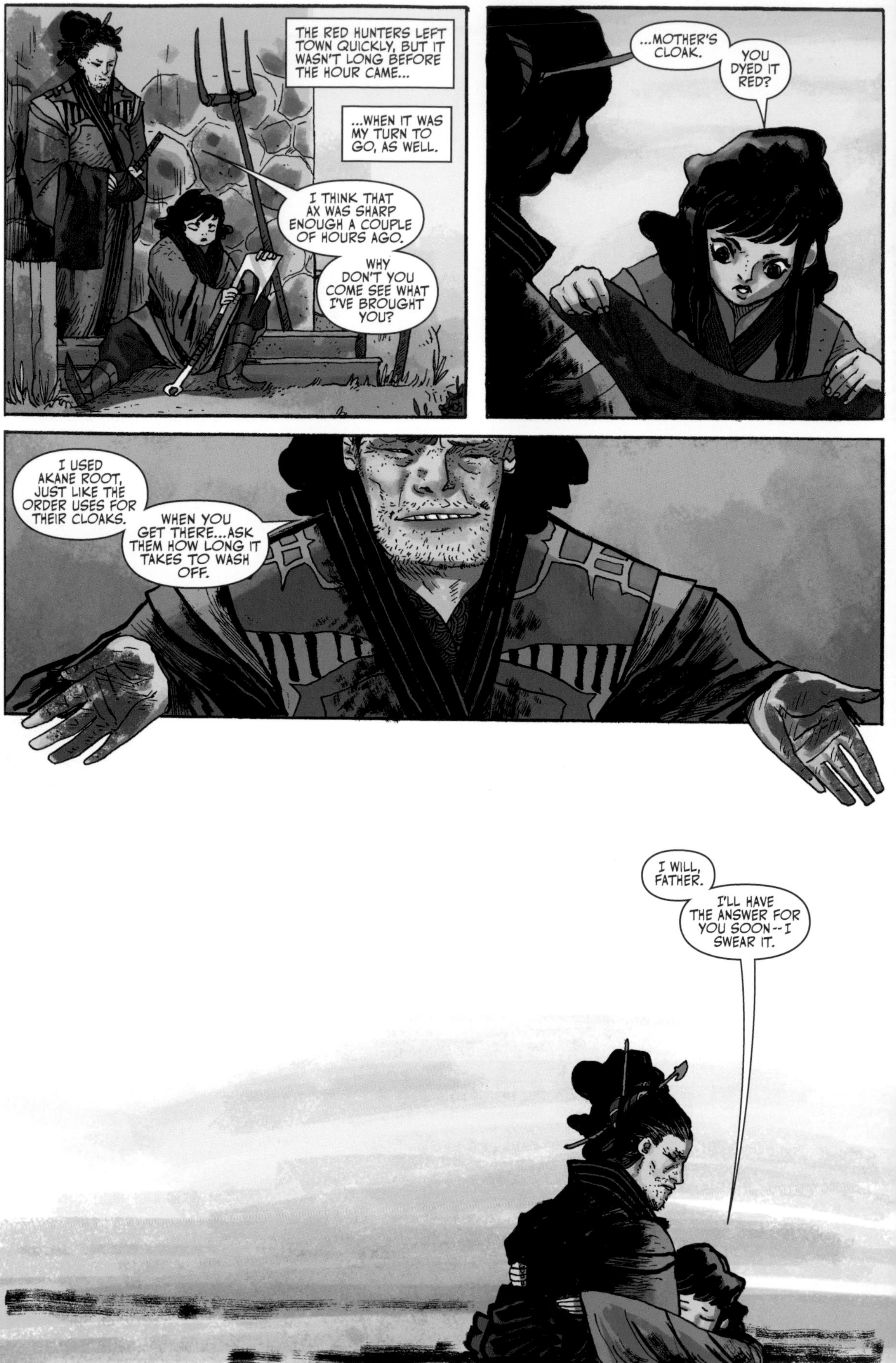
THE RED HUNTERS LEFT TOWN QUICKLY, BUT IT WASN'T LONG BEFORE THE HOUR CAME...
...WHEN IT WAS MY TURN TO GO, AS WELL.
I THINK THAT AX WAS SHARP ENOUGH A COUPLE OF HOURS AGO.
WHY DON'T YOU COME SEE WHAT I'VE BROUGHT YOU?
...MOTHER'S CLOAK.
YOU DYED IT RED?
I USED AKANE ROOT, JUST LIKE THE ORDER USES FOR THEIR CLOAKS.
WHEN YOU GET THERE...ASK THEM HOW LONG IT TAKES TO WASH OFF.
I WILL, FATHER.
I'LL HAVE THE ANSWER FOR YOU SOON--I SWEAR IT.

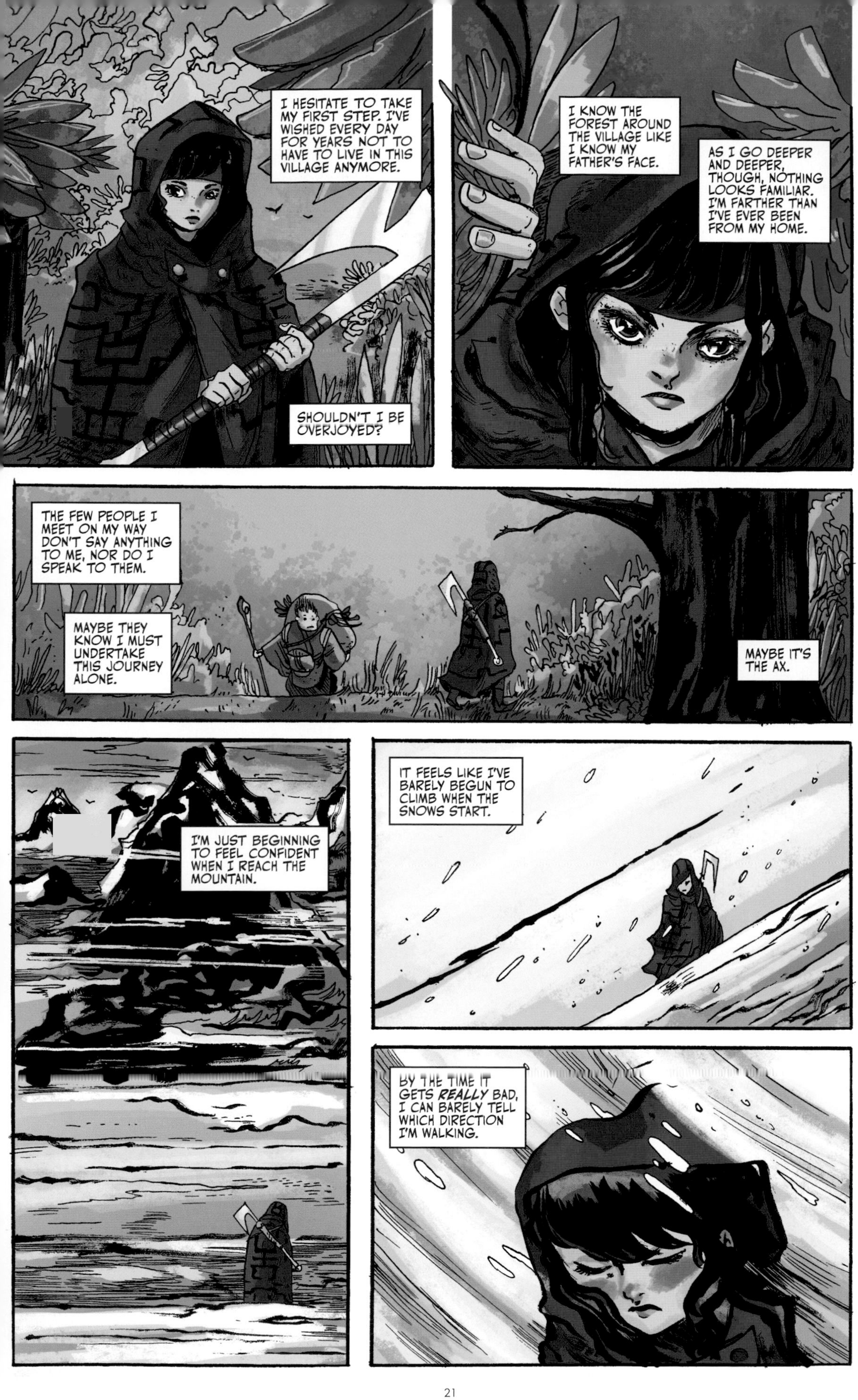
I HESITATE TO TAKE MY FIRST STEP. I'VE WISHED EVERY DAY FOR YEARS NOT TO HAVE TO LIVE IN THIS VILLAGE ANYMORE.
SHOULDN'T I BE OVERJOYED?
I KNOW THE FOREST AROUND THE VILLAGE LIKE I KNOW MY FATHER'S FACE.
AS I GO DEEPER AND DEEPER, THOUGH, NOTHING LOOKS FAMILIAR. I'M FARTHER THAN I'VE EVER BEEN FROM MY HOME.
THE FEW PEOPLE I MEET ON MY WAY DON'T SAY ANYTHING TO ME, NOR DO I SPEAK TO THEM.
MAYBE THEY KNOW I MUST UNDERTAKE THIS JOURNEY ALONE.
MAYBE IT'S THE AX.
I'M JUST BEGINNING TO FEEL CONFIDENT WHEN I REACH THE MOUNTAIN.
IT FEELS LIKE I'VE BARELY BEGUN TO CLIMB WHEN THE SNOWS START.
BY THE TIME IT GETS *REALLY* BAD, I CAN BARELY TELL WHICH DIRECTION I'M WALKING.

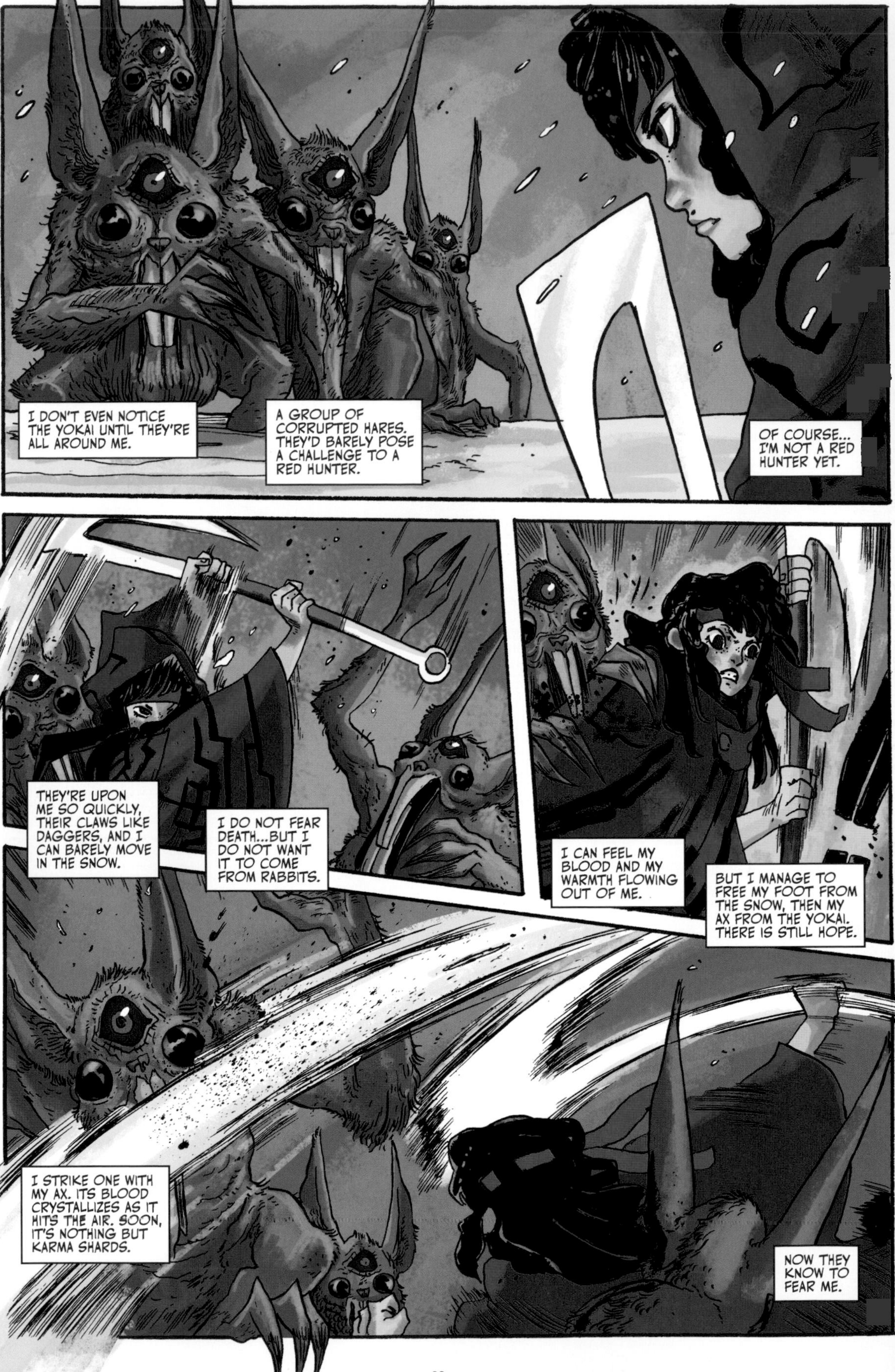
I DON'T EVEN NOTICE THE YOKAI UNTIL THEY'RE ALL AROUND ME.
A GROUP OF CORRUPTED HARES. THEY'D BARELY POSE A CHALLENGE TO A RED HUNTER.
OF COURSE... I'M NOT A RED HUNTER YET.
THEY'RE UPON ME SO QUICKLY, THEIR CLAWS LIKE DAGGERS, AND I CAN BARELY MOVE IN THE SNOW.
I DO NOT FEAR DEATH...BUT I DO NOT WANT IT TO COME FROM RABBITS.
I CAN FEEL MY BLOOD AND MY WARMTH FLOWING OUT OF ME.
BUT I MANAGE TO FREE MY FOOT FROM THE SNOW, THEN MY AX FROM THE YOKAI. THERE IS STILL HOPE.
I STRIKE ONE WITH MY AX. ITS BLOOD CRYSTALLIZES AS IT HITS THE AIR. SOON, IT'S NOTHING BUT KARMA SHARDS.
NOW THEY KNOW TO FEAR ME.

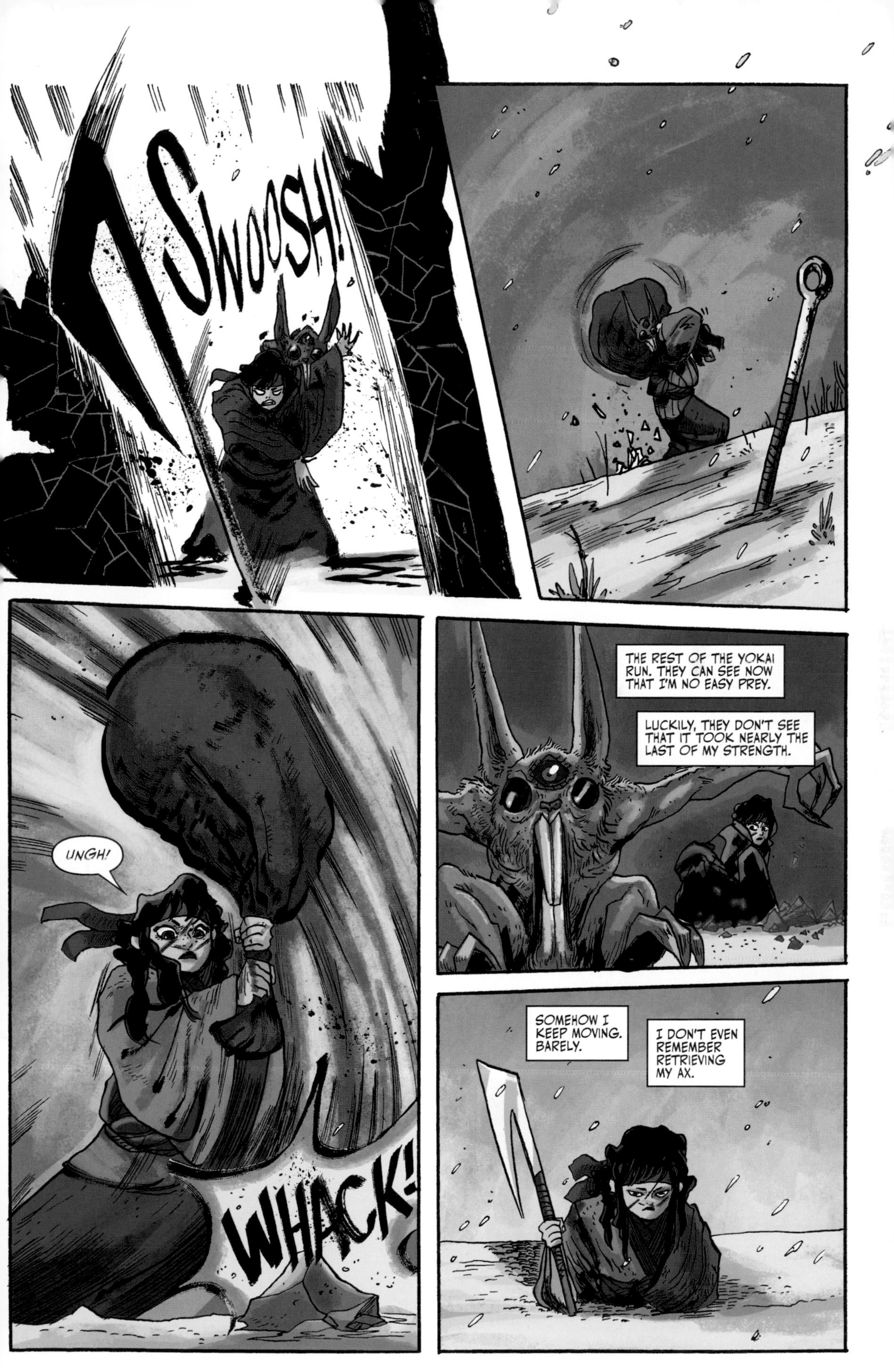
SWOOSH!
UNGH!
WHACK!
THE REST OF THE YOKAI RUN. THEY CAN SEE NOW THAT I'M NO EASY PREY.
LUCKILY, THEY DON'T SEE THAT IT TOOK NEARLY THE LAST OF MY STRENGTH.
SOMEHOW I KEEP MOVING. BARELY.
I DON'T EVEN REMEMBER RETRIEVING MY AX.

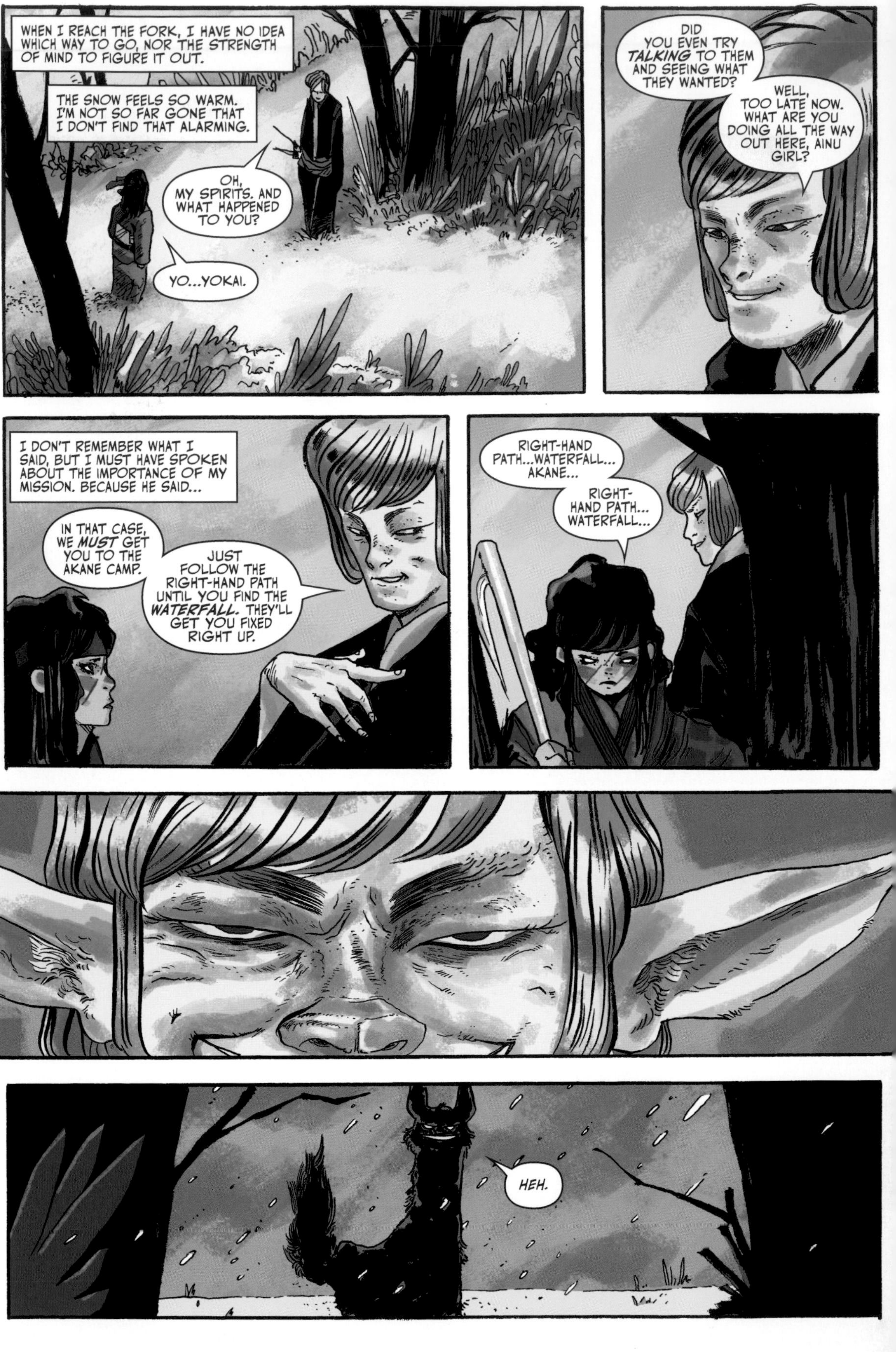
WHEN I REACH THE FORK, I HAVE NO IDEA WHICH WAY TO GO, NOR THE STRENGTH OF MIND TO FIGURE IT OUT.
THE SNOW FEELS SO WARM. I'M NOT SO FAR GONE THAT I DON'T FIND THAT ALARMING.
OH, MY SPIRITS. AND WHAT HAPPENED TO YOU?
YO...YOKAI.
DID YOU EVEN TRY *TALKING* TO THEM AND SEEING WHAT THEY WANTED?
WELL, TOO LATE NOW. WHAT ARE YOU DOING ALL THE WAY OUT HERE, AINU GIRL?
I DON'T REMEMBER WHAT I SAID, BUT I MUST HAVE SPOKEN ABOUT THE IMPORTANCE OF MY MISSION. BECAUSE HE SAID...
IN THAT CASE, WE *MUST* GET YOU TO THE AKANE CAMP.
JUST FOLLOW THE RIGHT-HAND PATH UNTIL YOU FIND THE *WATERFALL.* THEY'LL GET YOU FIXED RIGHT UP.
RIGHT-HAND PATH...WATERFALL... AKANE...
RIGHT-HAND PATH... WATERFALL...
HEH.

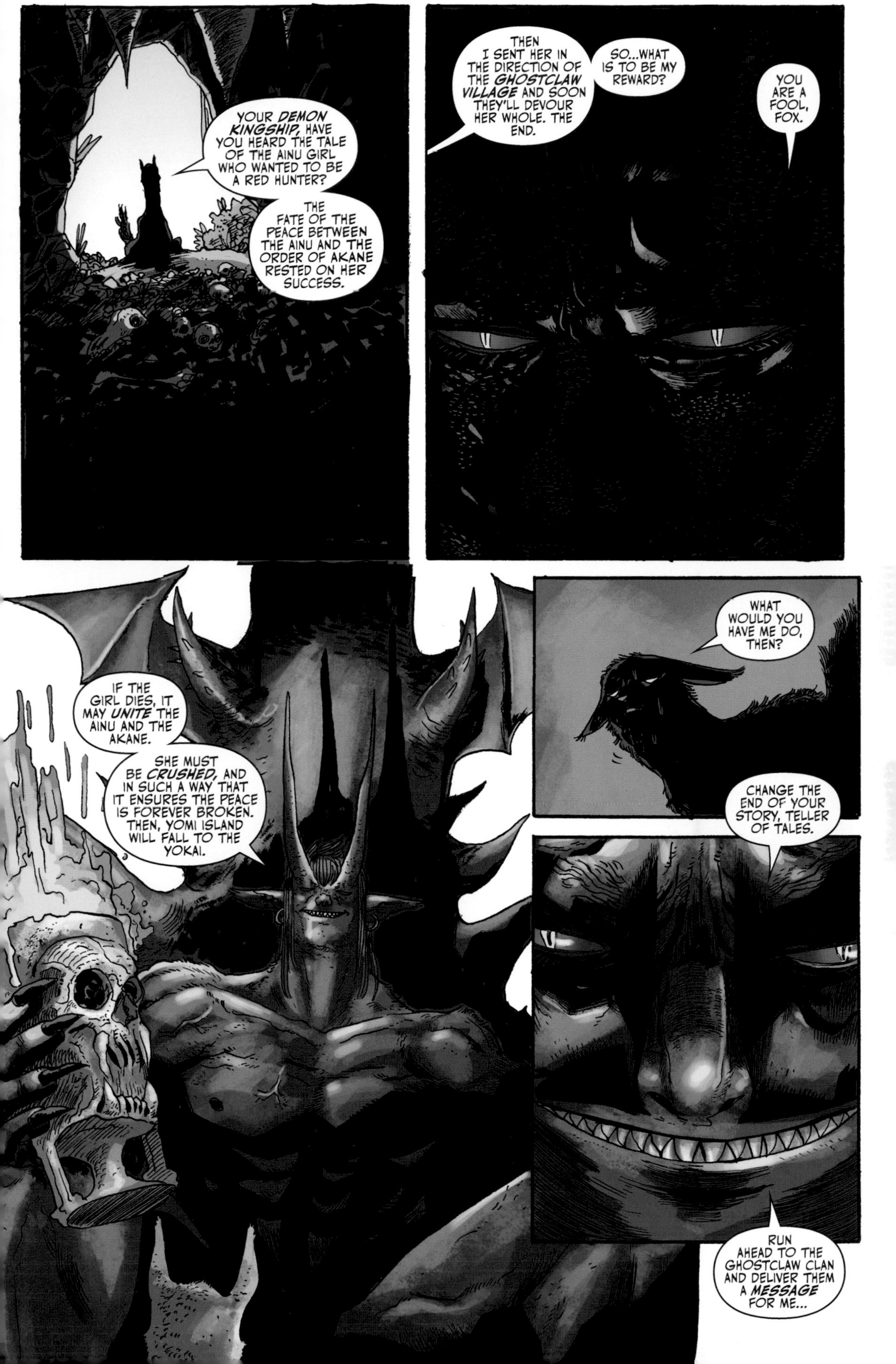
YOUR DEMON KINGSHIP, HAVE YOU HEARD THE TALE OF THE AINU GIRL WHO WANTED TO BE A RED HUNTER?
THE FATE OF THE PEACE BETWEEN THE AINU AND THE ORDER OF AKANE RESTED ON HER SUCCESS.
THEN I SENT HER IN THE DIRECTION OF THE GHOSTCLAW VILLAGE AND SOON THEY'LL DEVOUR HER WHOLE. THE END.
SO...WHAT IS TO BE MY REWARD?
YOU ARE A FOOL, FOX.
IF THE GIRL DIES, IT MAY UNITE THE AINU AND THE AKANE.
SHE MUST BE CRUSHED, AND IN SUCH A WAY THAT IT ENSURES THE PEACE IS FOREVER BROKEN. THEN, YOMI ISLAND WILL FALL TO THE YOKAI.
WHAT WOULD YOU HAVE ME DO, THEN?
CHANGE THE END OF YOUR STORY, TELLER OF TALES.
RUN AHEAD TO THE GHOSTCLAW CLAN AND DELIVER THEM A MESSAGE FOR ME...

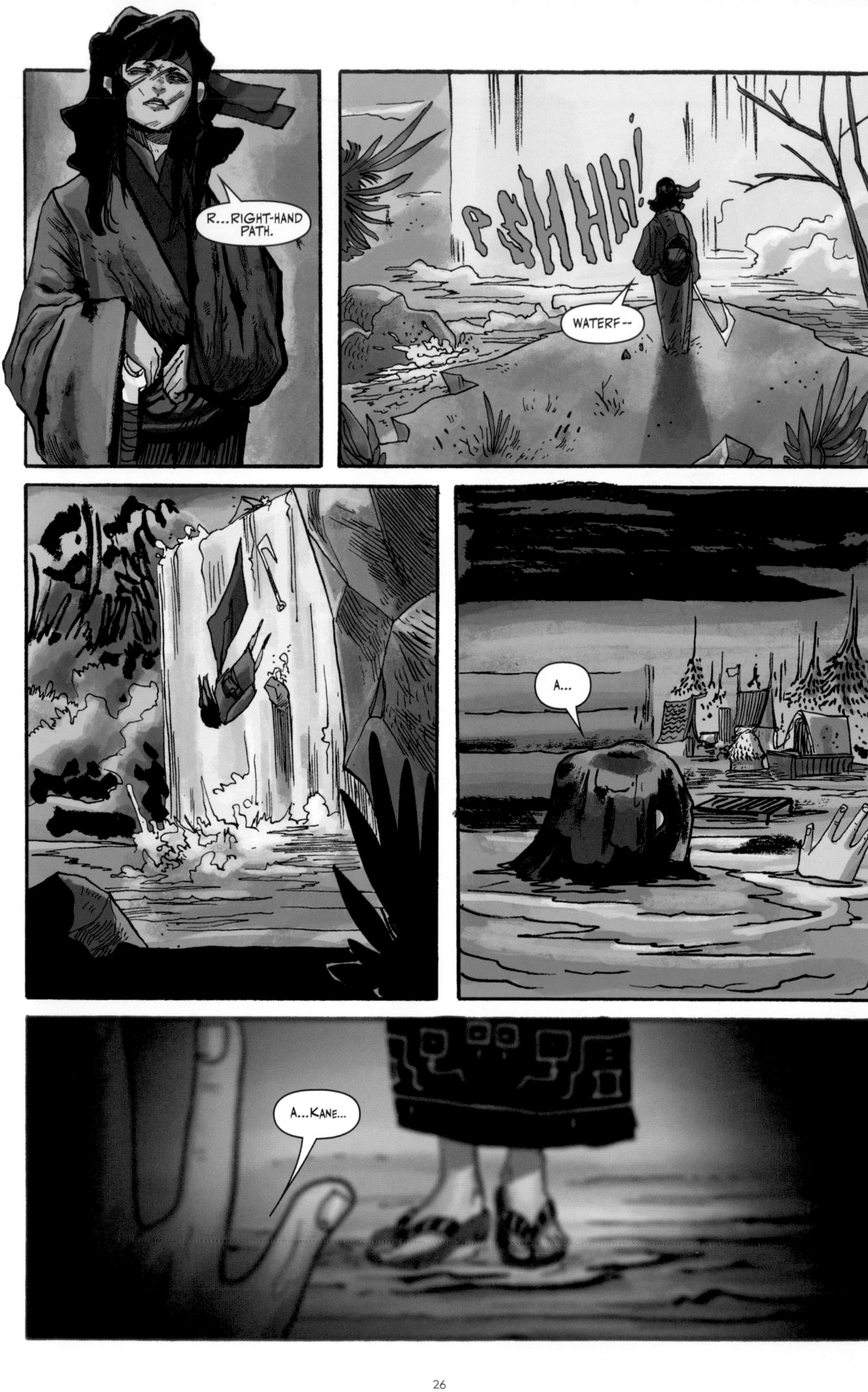
R...RIGHT-HAND PATH.
PSHHH!
WATERF--
A...
A...KANE...

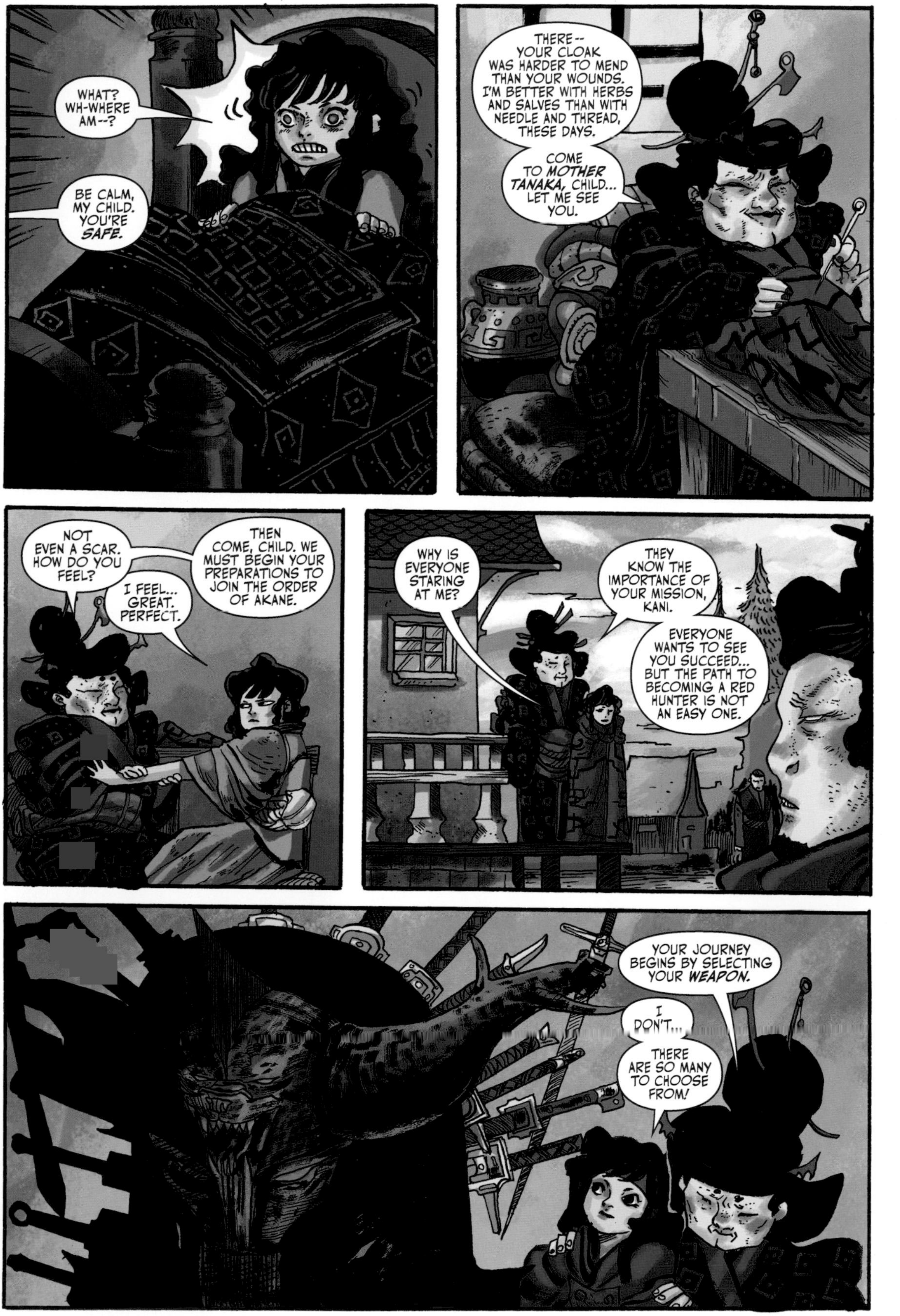
WHAT? WH-WHERE AM--?
BE CALM, MY CHILD. YOU'RE *SAFE.*
THERE-- YOUR CLOAK WAS HARDER TO MEND THAN YOUR WOUNDS. I'M BETTER WITH HERBS AND SALVES THAN WITH NEEDLE AND THREAD, THESE DAYS.
COME TO *MOTHER TANAKA,* CHILD... LET ME SEE YOU.
NOT EVEN A SCAR. HOW DO YOU FEEL?
I FEEL... GREAT. PERFECT.
THEN COME, CHILD. WE MUST BEGIN YOUR PREPARATIONS TO JOIN THE ORDER OF AKANE.
WHY IS EVERYONE STARING AT ME?
THEY KNOW THE IMPORTANCE OF YOUR MISSION, KANI.
EVERYONE WANTS TO SEE YOU SUCCEED... BUT THE PATH TO BECOMING A RED HUNTER IS NOT AN EASY ONE.
YOUR JOURNEY BEGINS BY SELECTING YOUR *WEAPON.*
I DON'T...
THERE ARE SO MANY TO CHOOSE FROM!

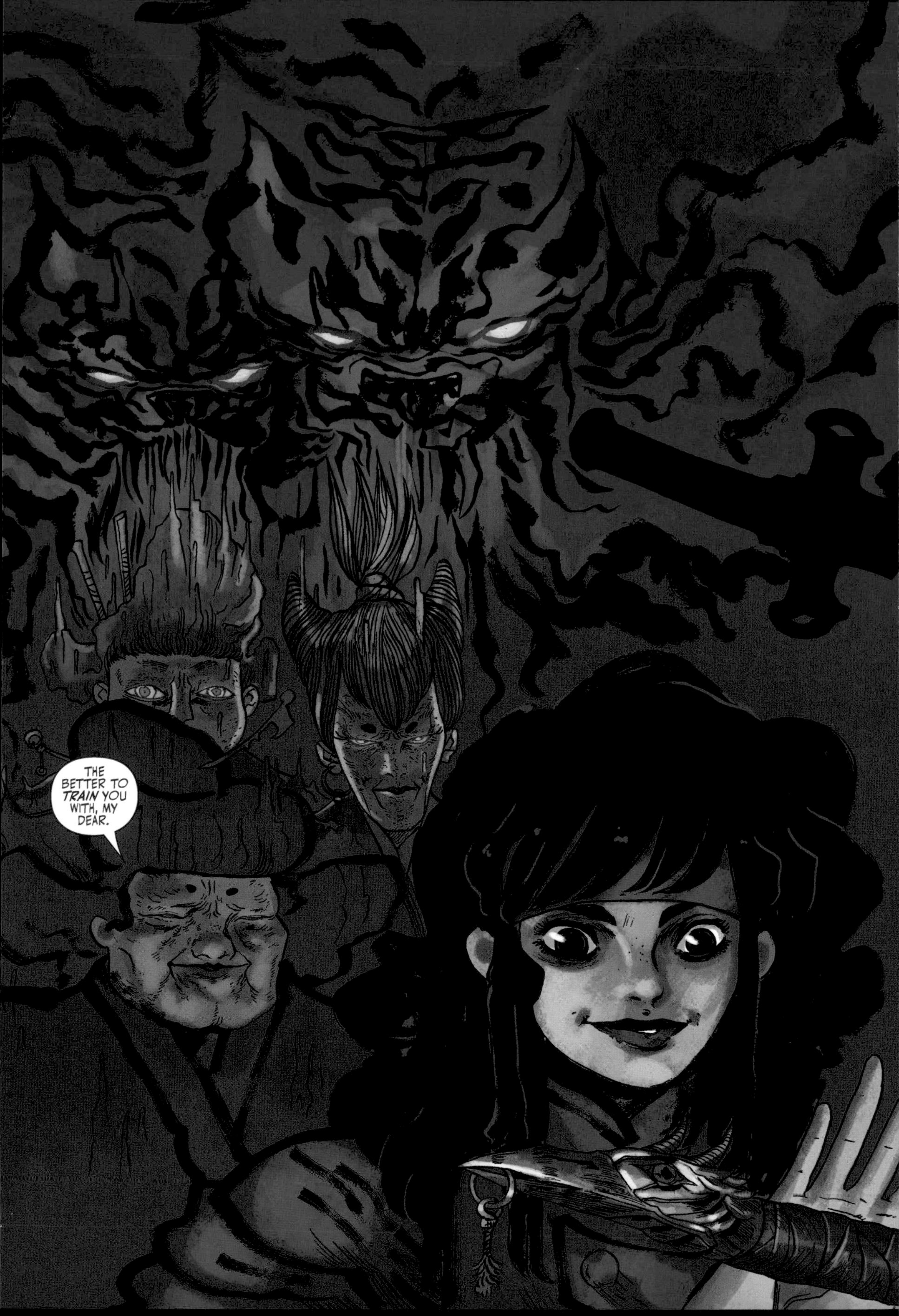
THE BETTER TO TRAIN YOU WITH, MY DEAR.

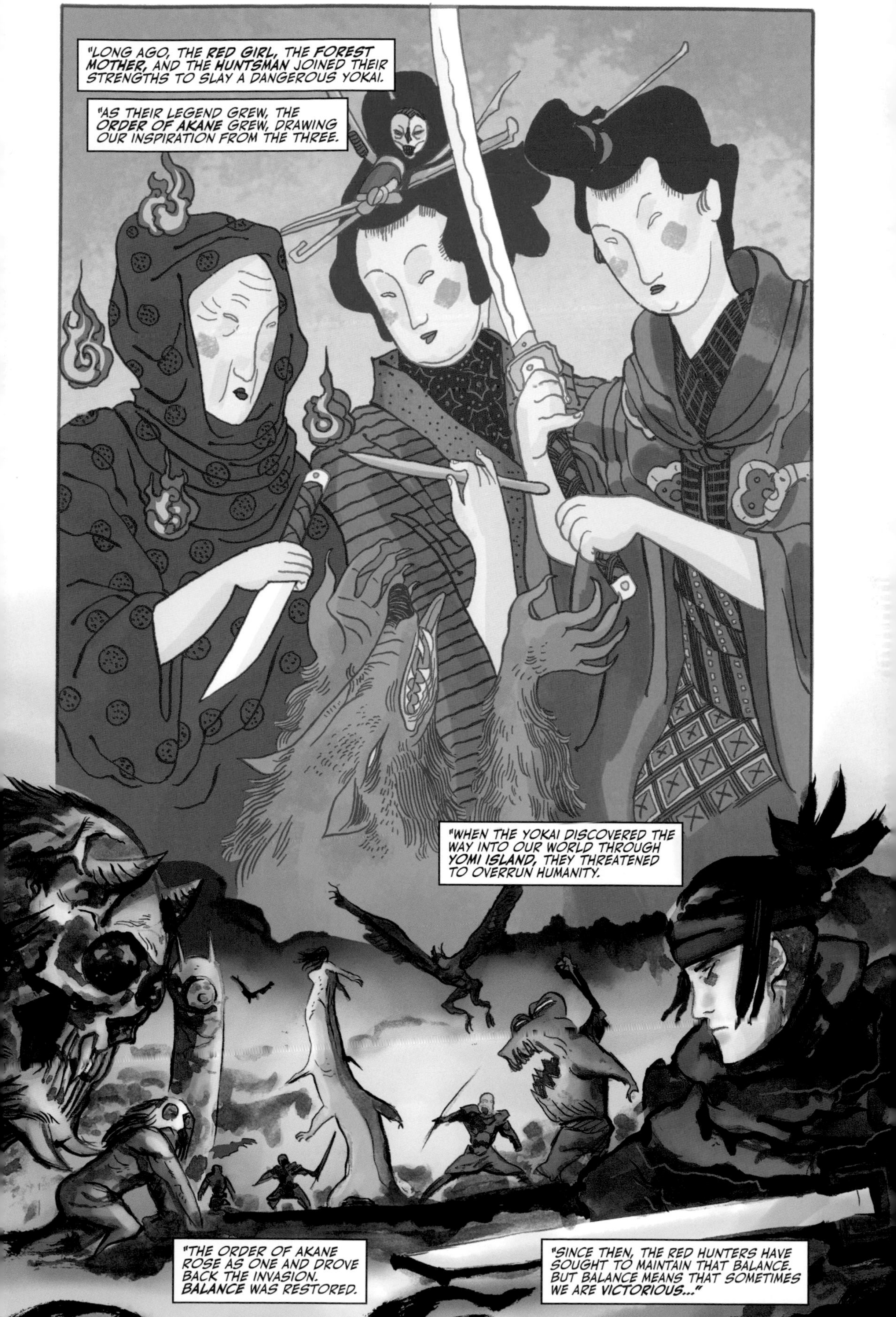
"LONG AGO, THE RED GIRL, THE FOREST MOTHER, AND THE HUNTSMAN JOINED THEIR STRENGTHS TO SLAY A DANGEROUS YOKAI.
"AS THEIR LEGEND GREW, THE ORDER OF AKANE GREW, DRAWING OUR INSPIRATION FROM THE THREE.
"WHEN THE YOKAI DISCOVERED THE WAY INTO OUR WORLD THROUGH YOMI ISLAND, THEY THREATENED TO OVERRUN HUMANITY.
"THE ORDER OF AKANE ROSE AS ONE AND DROVE BACK THE INVASION. BALANCE WAS RESTORED.
"SINCE THEN, THE RED HUNTERS HAVE SOUGHT TO MAINTAIN THAT BALANCE. BUT BALANCE MEANS THAT SOMETIMES WE ARE VICTORIOUS..."

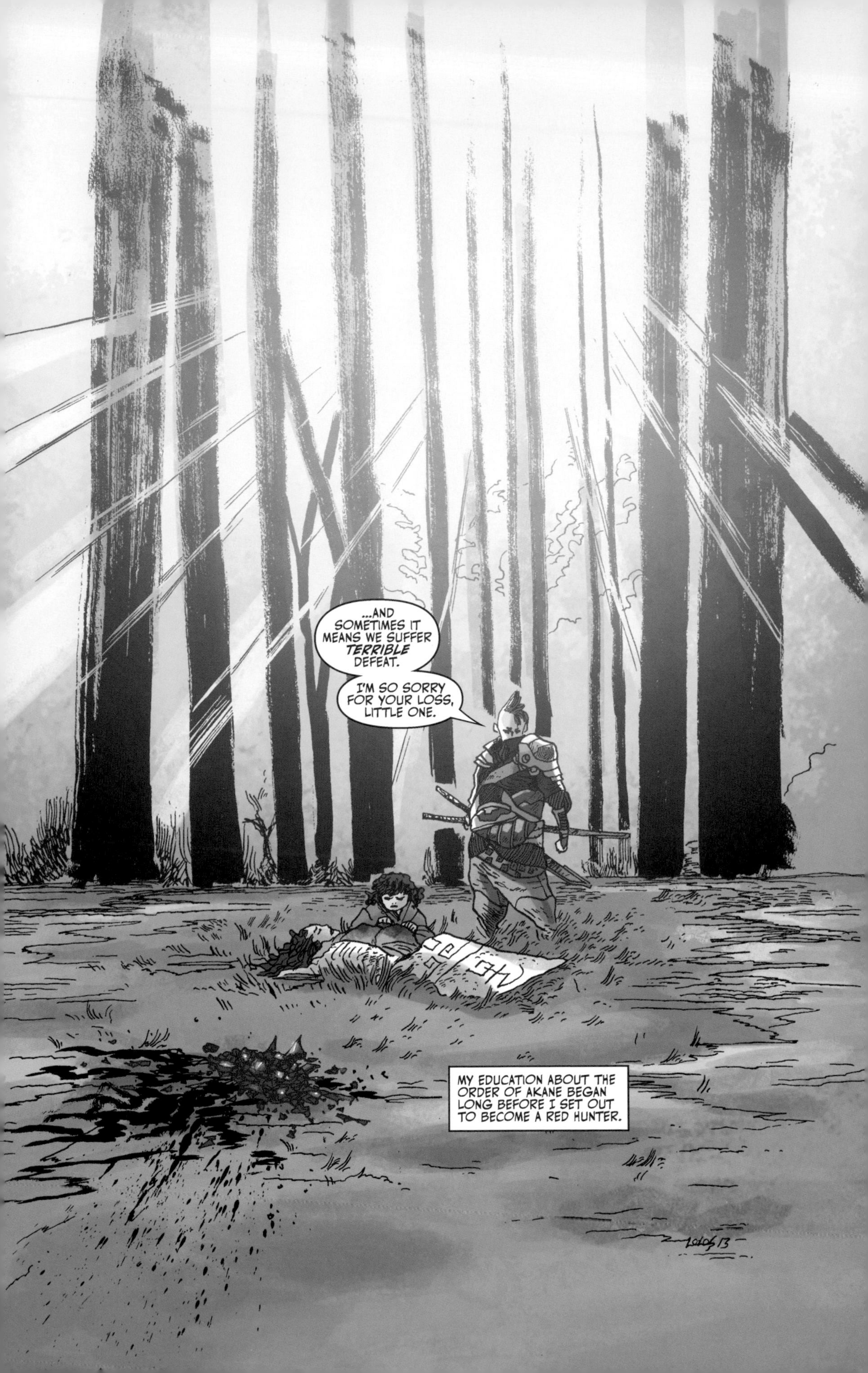
...AND SOMETIMES IT MEANS WE SUFFER *TERRIBLE* DEFEAT.
I'M SO SORRY FOR YOUR LOSS, LITTLE ONE.
MY EDUCATION ABOUT THE ORDER OF AKANE BEGAN LONG BEFORE I SET OUT TO BECOME A RED HUNTER.

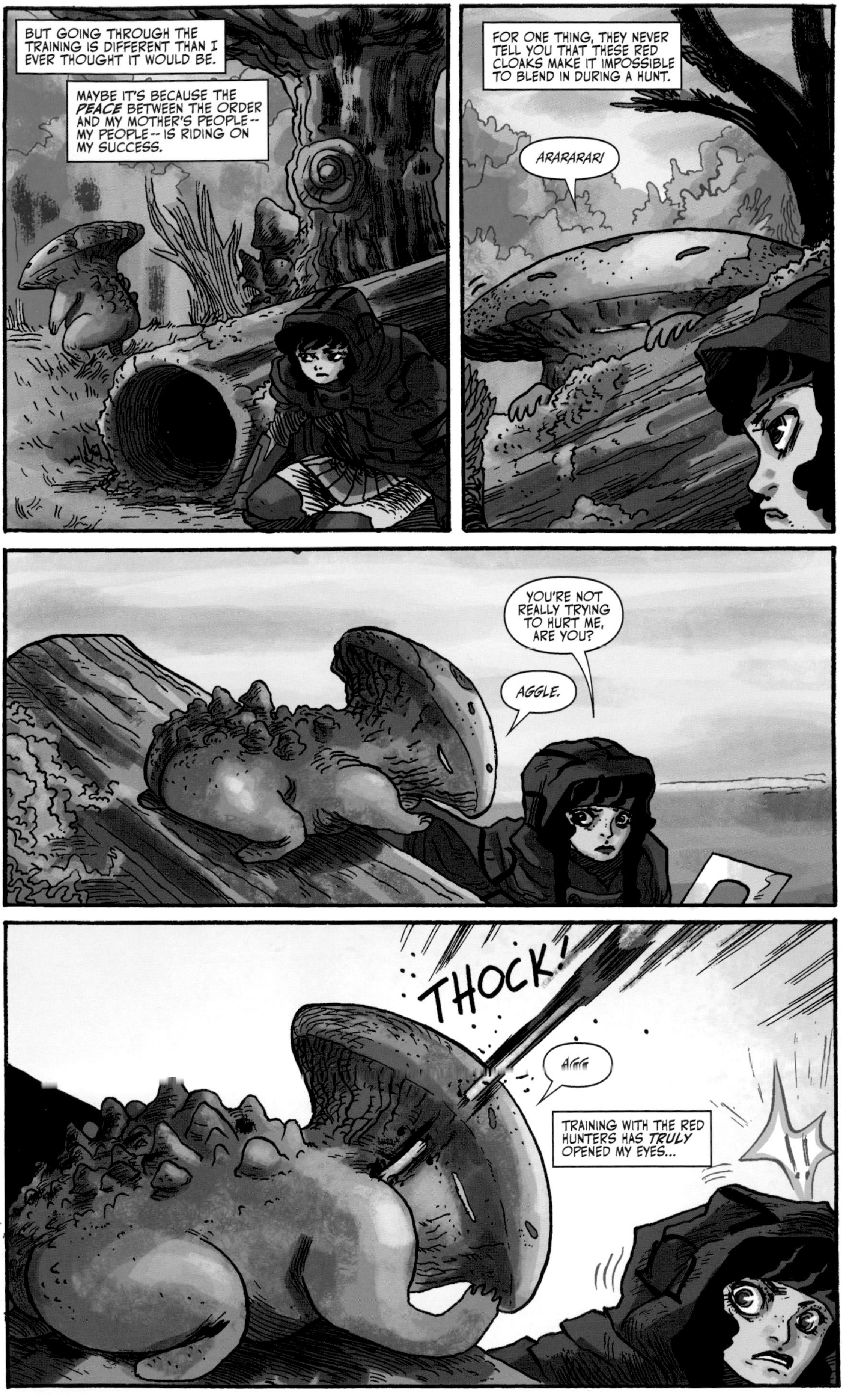
BUT GOING THROUGH THE TRAINING IS DIFFERENT THAN I EVER THOUGHT IT WOULD BE.
MAYBE IT'S BECAUSE THE PEACE BETWEEN THE ORDER AND MY MOTHER'S PEOPLE-- MY PEOPLE-- IS RIDING ON MY SUCCESS.
FOR ONE THING, THEY NEVER TELL YOU THAT THESE RED CLOAKS MAKE IT IMPOSSIBLE TO BLEND IN DURING A HUNT.
ARARARARI
YOU'RE NOT REALLY TRYING TO HURT ME, ARE YOU?
AGGLE.
THOCK!
AGG
TRAINING WITH THE RED HUNTERS HAS TRULY OPENED MY EYES...

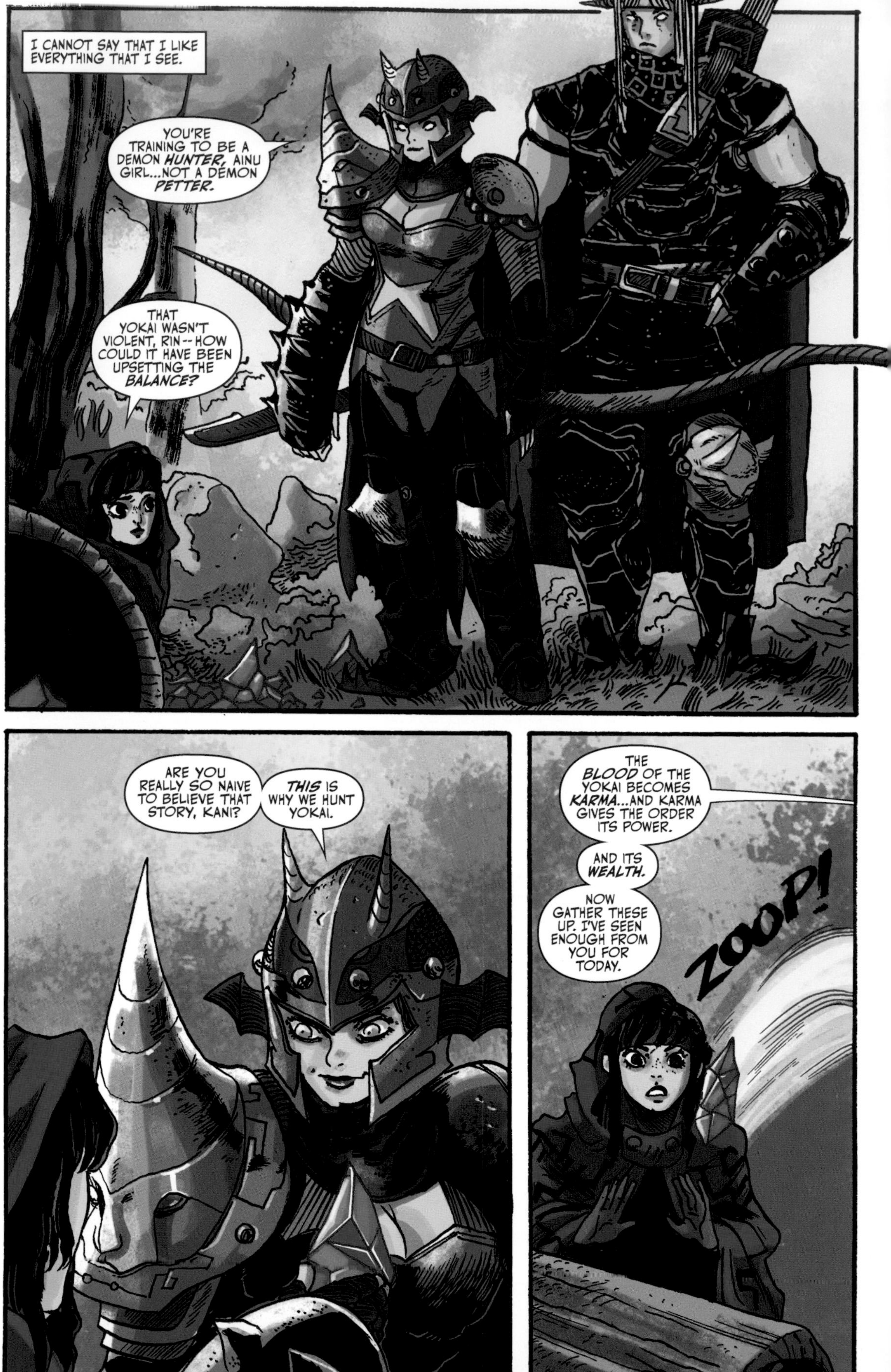

I CANNOT SAY THAT I LIKE EVERYTHING THAT I SEE.
YOU'RE TRAINING TO BE A DEMON HUNTER, AINU GIRL...NOT A DEMON PETTER.
THAT YOKAI WASN'T VIOLENT, RIN-- HOW COULD IT HAVE BEEN UPSETTING THE BALANCE?
ARE YOU REALLY SO NAIVE TO BELIEVE THAT STORY, KANI?
THIS IS WHY WE HUNT YOKAI.
THE BLOOD OF THE YOKAI BECOMES KARMA...AND KARMA GIVES THE ORDER ITS POWER.
AND ITS WEALTH.
NOW GATHER THESE UP. I'VE SEEN ENOUGH FROM YOU FOR TODAY.
ZOOP!

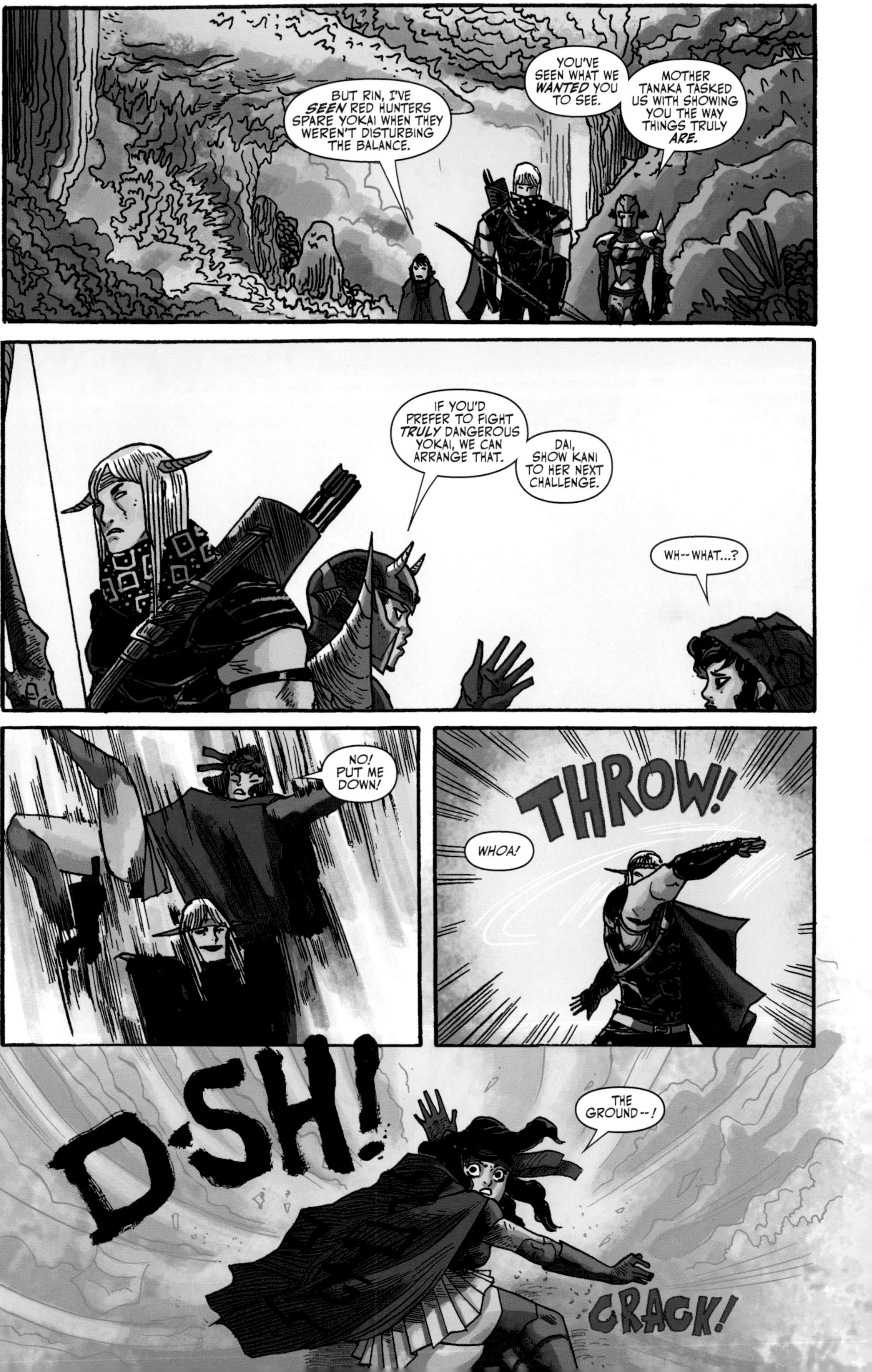
BUT RIN, I'VE SEEN RED HUNTERS SPARE YOKAI WHEN THEY WEREN'T DISTURBING THE BALANCE.
YOU'VE SEEN WHAT WE WANTED YOU TO SEE.
MOTHER TANAKA TASKED US WITH SHOWING YOU THE WAY THINGS TRULY ARE.
IF YOU'D PREFER TO FIGHT TRULY DANGEROUS YOKAI, WE CAN ARRANGE THAT.
DAI, SHOW KANI TO HER NEXT CHALLENGE.
WH--WHAT...?
NO! PUT ME DOWN!
THROW!
WHOA!
D-SH!
THE GROUND--!
CRACK!

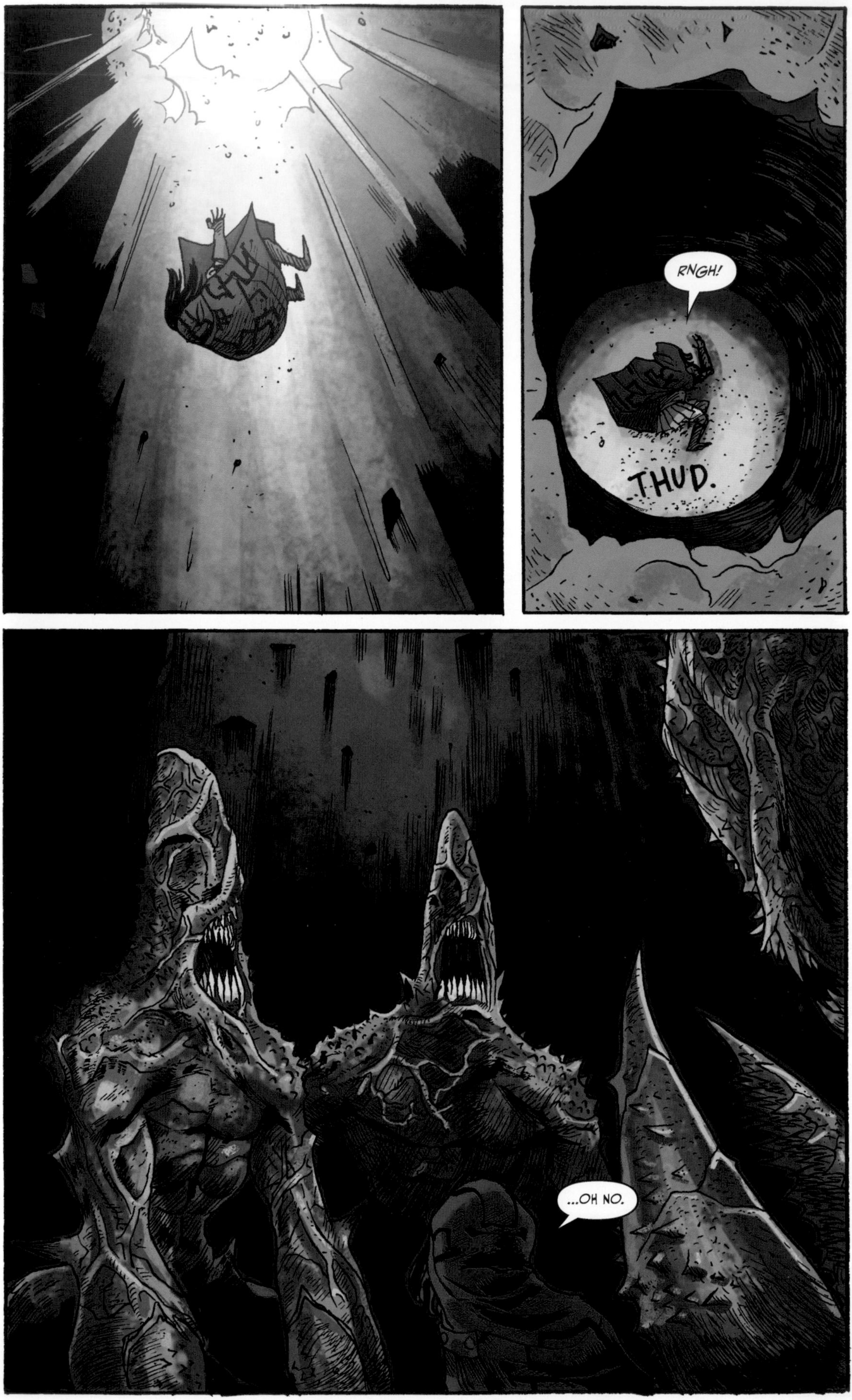
RNGH!
THUD.
...OH NO.

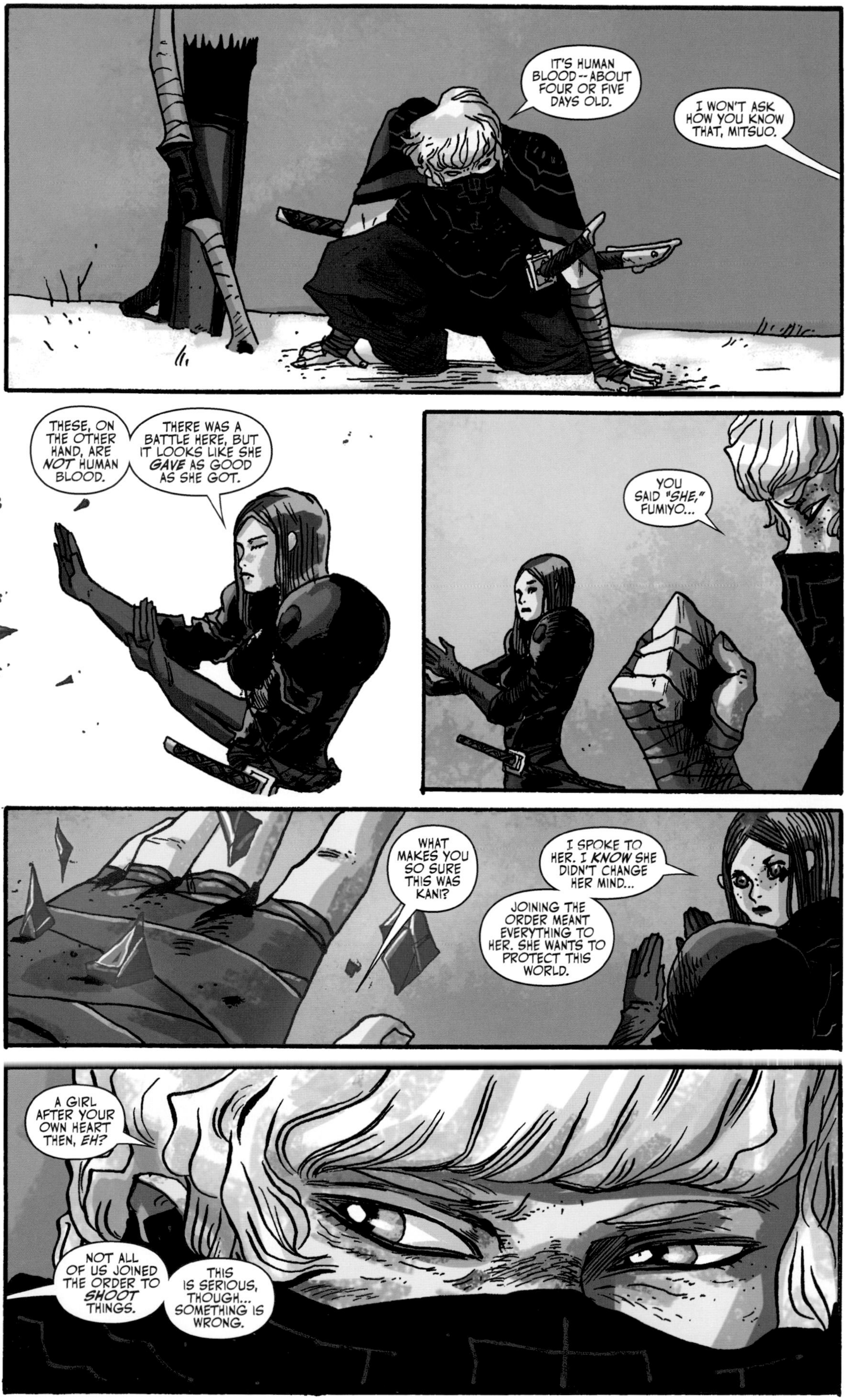
IT'S HUMAN BLOOD--ABOUT FOUR OR FIVE DAYS OLD.
I WON'T ASK HOW YOU KNOW THAT, MITSUO.
THESE, ON THE OTHER HAND, ARE NOT HUMAN BLOOD.
THERE WAS A BATTLE HERE, BUT IT LOOKS LIKE SHE GAVE AS GOOD AS SHE GOT.
YOU SAID "SHE," FUMIYO...
WHAT MAKES YOU SO SURE THIS WAS KANI?
I SPOKE TO HER. I KNOW SHE DIDN'T CHANGE HER MIND...
JOINING THE ORDER MEANT EVERYTHING TO HER. SHE WANTS TO PROTECT THIS WORLD.
A GIRL AFTER YOUR OWN HEART THEN, EH?
NOT ALL OF US JOINED THE ORDER TO SHOOT THINGS.
THIS IS SERIOUS, THOUGH... SOMETHING IS WRONG.

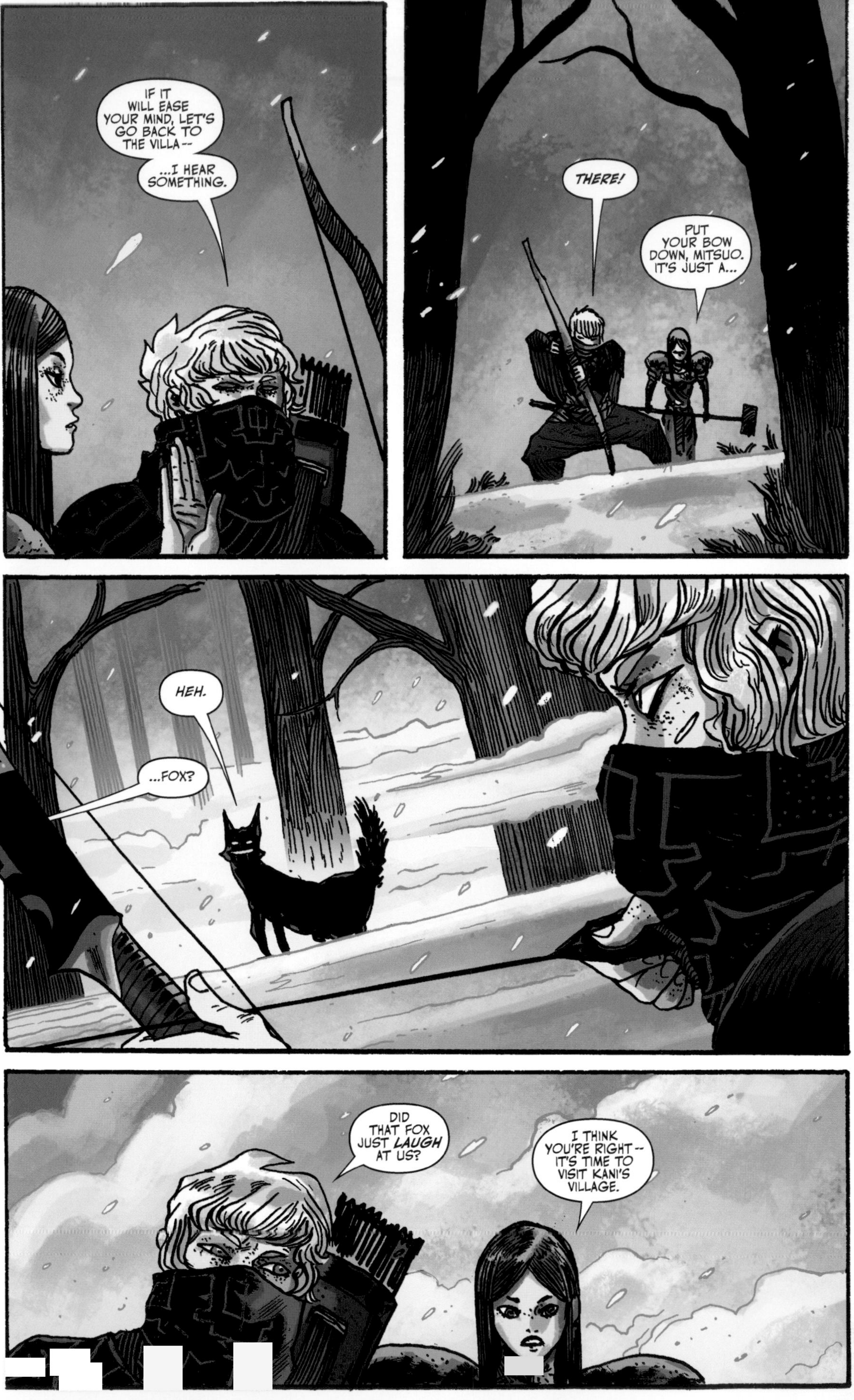
IF IT WILL EASE YOUR MIND, LET'S GO BACK TO THE VILLA--
...I HEAR SOMETHING.
THERE!
PUT YOUR BOW DOWN, MITSUO. IT'S JUST A...
HEH.
...FOX?
DID THAT FOX JUST LAUGH AT US?
I THINK YOU'RE RIGHT-- IT'S TIME TO VISIT KANI'S VILLAGE.

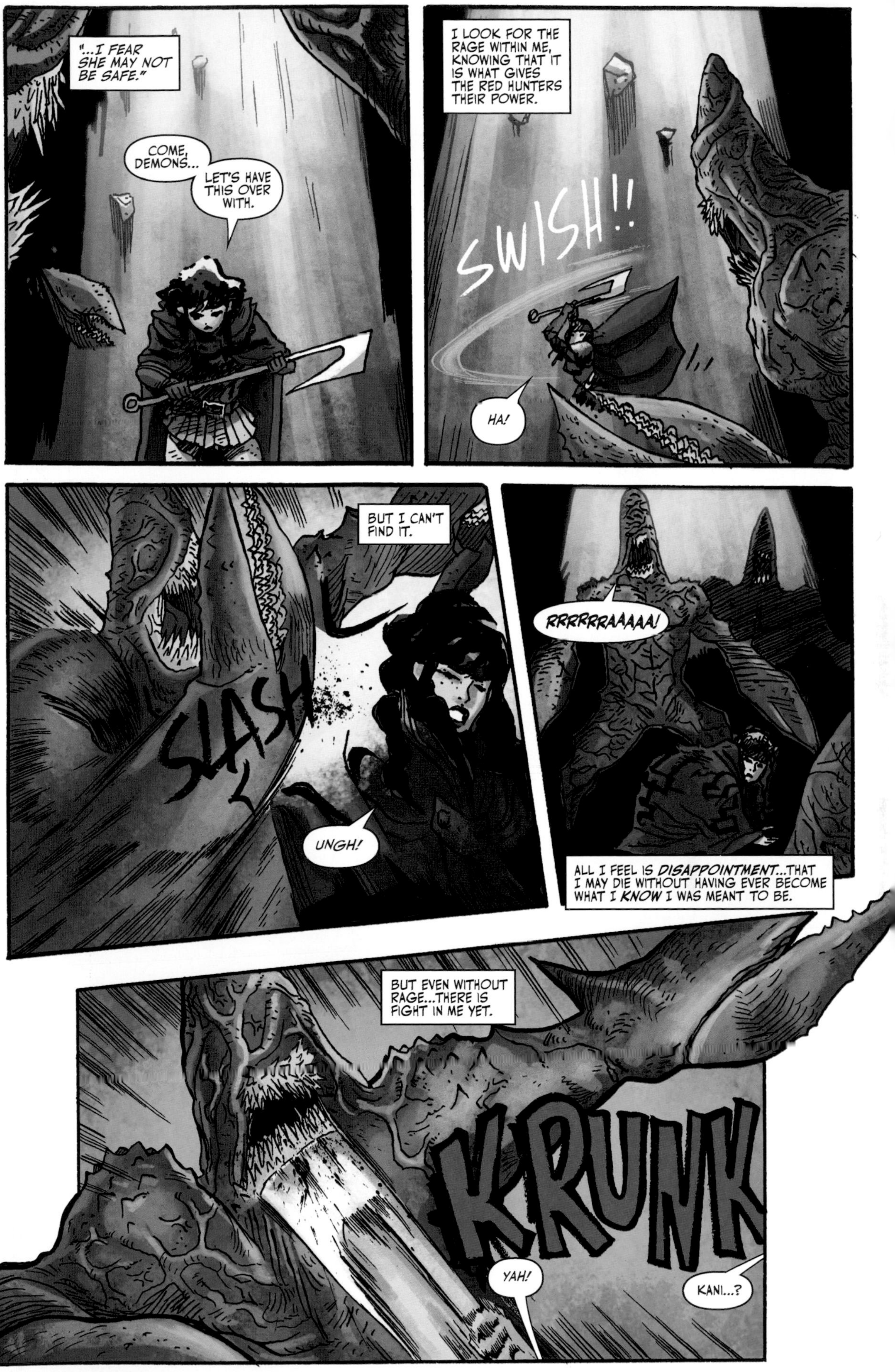
"...I FEAR SHE MAY NOT BE SAFE."
COME, DEMONS...
LET'S HAVE THIS OVER WITH.
I LOOK FOR THE RAGE WITHIN ME, KNOWING THAT IT IS WHAT GIVES THE RED HUNTERS THEIR POWER.
SWISH!!
HA!
BUT I CAN'T FIND IT.
SLASH
UNGH!
RRRRRRAAAAA!
ALL I FEEL IS DISAPPOINTMENT...THAT I MAY DIE WITHOUT HAVING EVER BECOME WHAT I KNOW I WAS MEANT TO BE.
BUT EVEN WITHOUT RAGE...THERE IS FIGHT IN ME YET.
KRUNK
YAH!
KANI...?

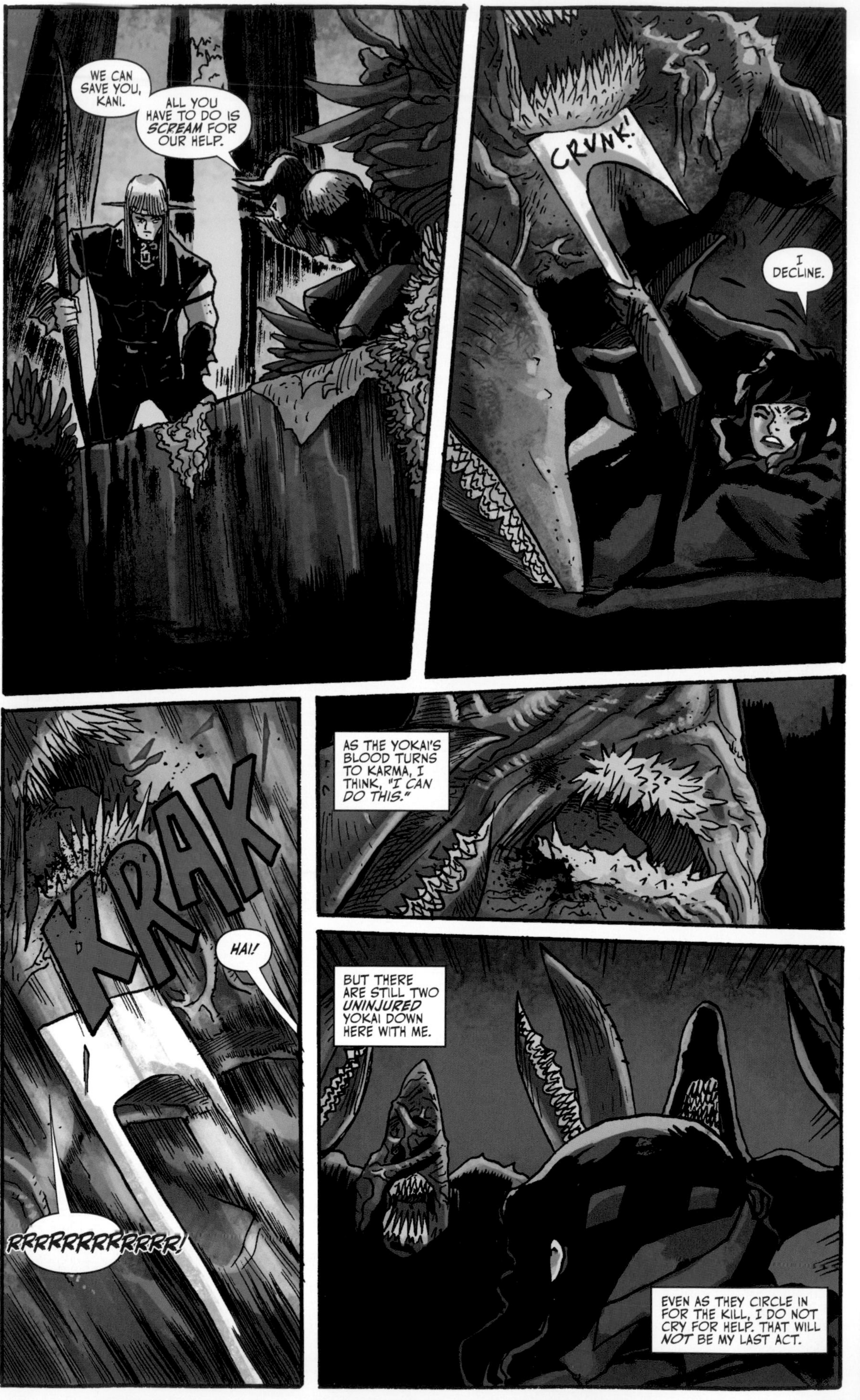
WE CAN SAVE YOU, KANI.
ALL YOU HAVE TO DO IS SCREAM FOR OUR HELP.
CRUNK!
I DECLINE.
KRAK
HAI!
RRRRRRRRRRRR!
AS THE YOKAI'S BLOOD TURNS TO KARMA, I THINK, "I CAN DO THIS."
BUT THERE ARE STILL TWO UNINJURED YOKAI DOWN HERE WITH ME.
EVEN AS THEY CIRCLE IN FOR THE KILL, I DO NOT CRY FOR HELP. THAT WILL NOT BE MY LAST ACT.

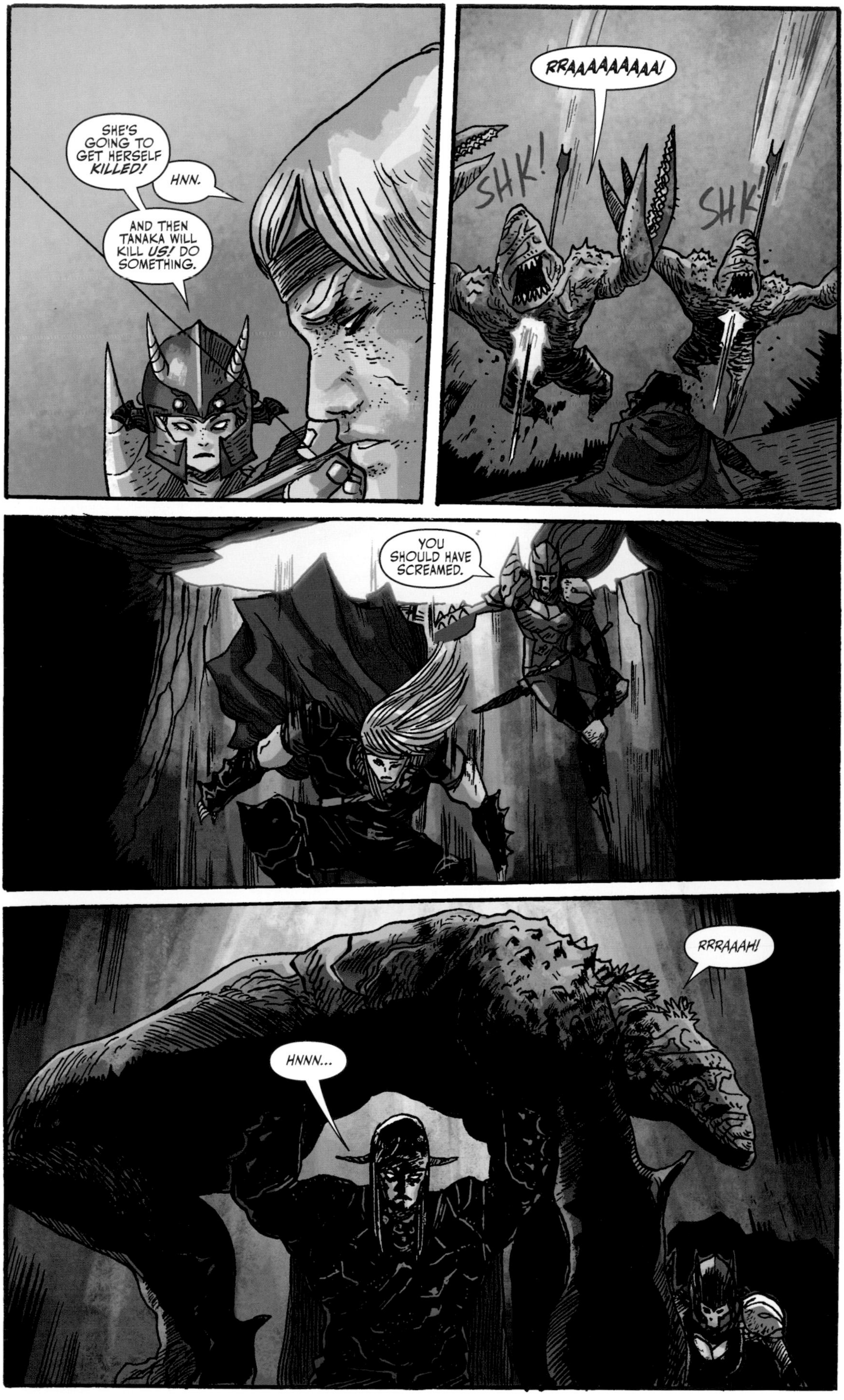
SHE'S GOING TO GET HERSELF *KILLED!*
HNN.
AND THEN TANAKA WILL KILL *US!* DO SOMETHING.
RRAAAAAAAAA!
SHK!
SHK
YOU SHOULD HAVE SCREAMED.
RRRAAAH!
HNNN...

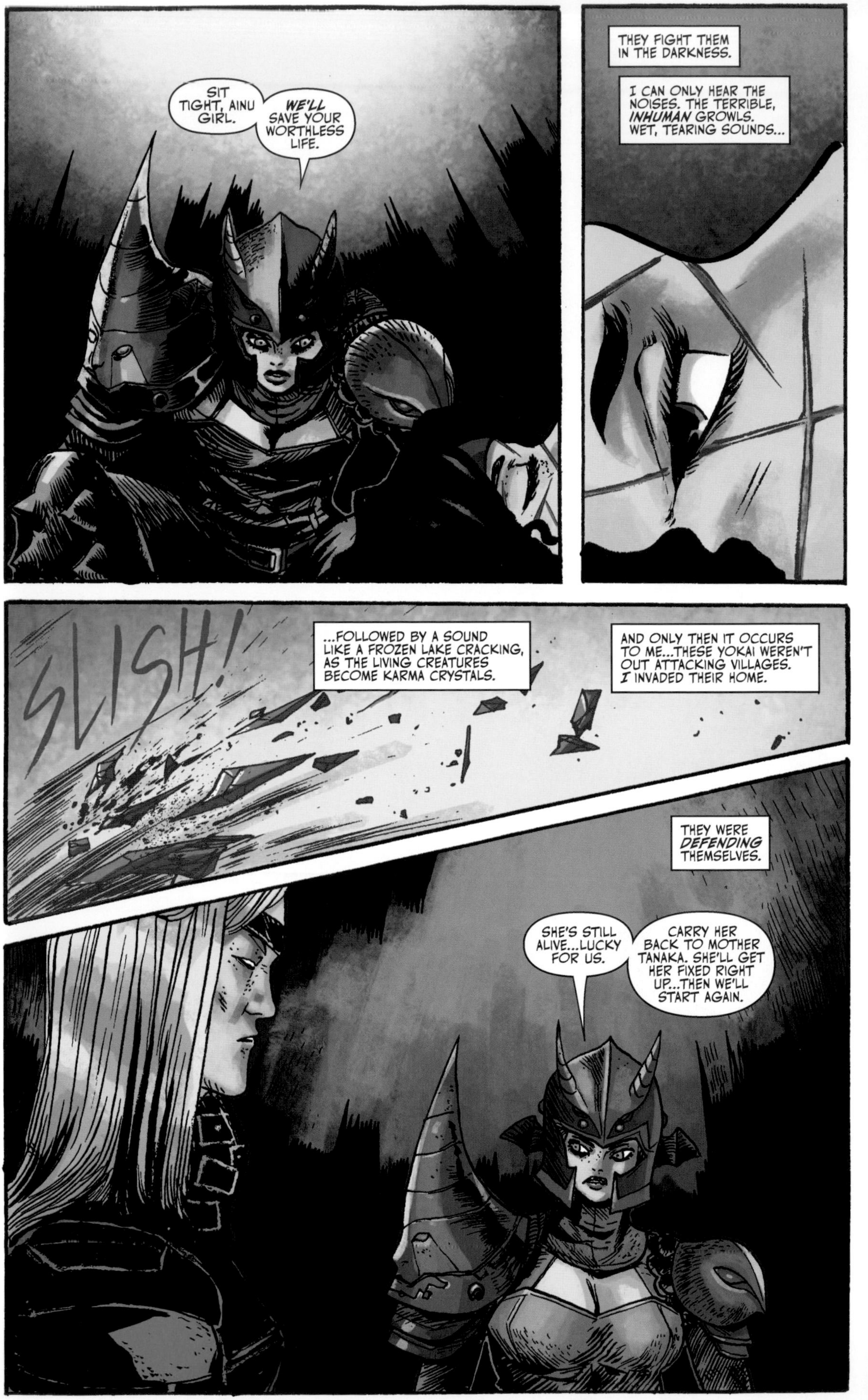
SIT TIGHT, AINU GIRL.
WE'LL SAVE YOUR WORTHLESS LIFE.
THEY FIGHT THEM IN THE DARKNESS.
I CAN ONLY HEAR THE NOISES. THE TERRIBLE, INHUMAN GROWLS. WET, TEARING SOUNDS...
SLISH!
...FOLLOWED BY A SOUND LIKE A FROZEN LAKE CRACKING, AS THE LIVING CREATURES BECOME KARMA CRYSTALS.
AND ONLY THEN IT OCCURS TO ME...THESE YOKAI WEREN'T OUT ATTACKING VILLAGES. I INVADED THEIR HOME.
THEY WERE DEFENDING THEMSELVES.
SHE'S STILL ALIVE...LUCKY FOR US.
CARRY HER BACK TO MOTHER TANAKA. SHE'LL GET HER FIXED RIGHT UP...THEN WE'LL START AGAIN.

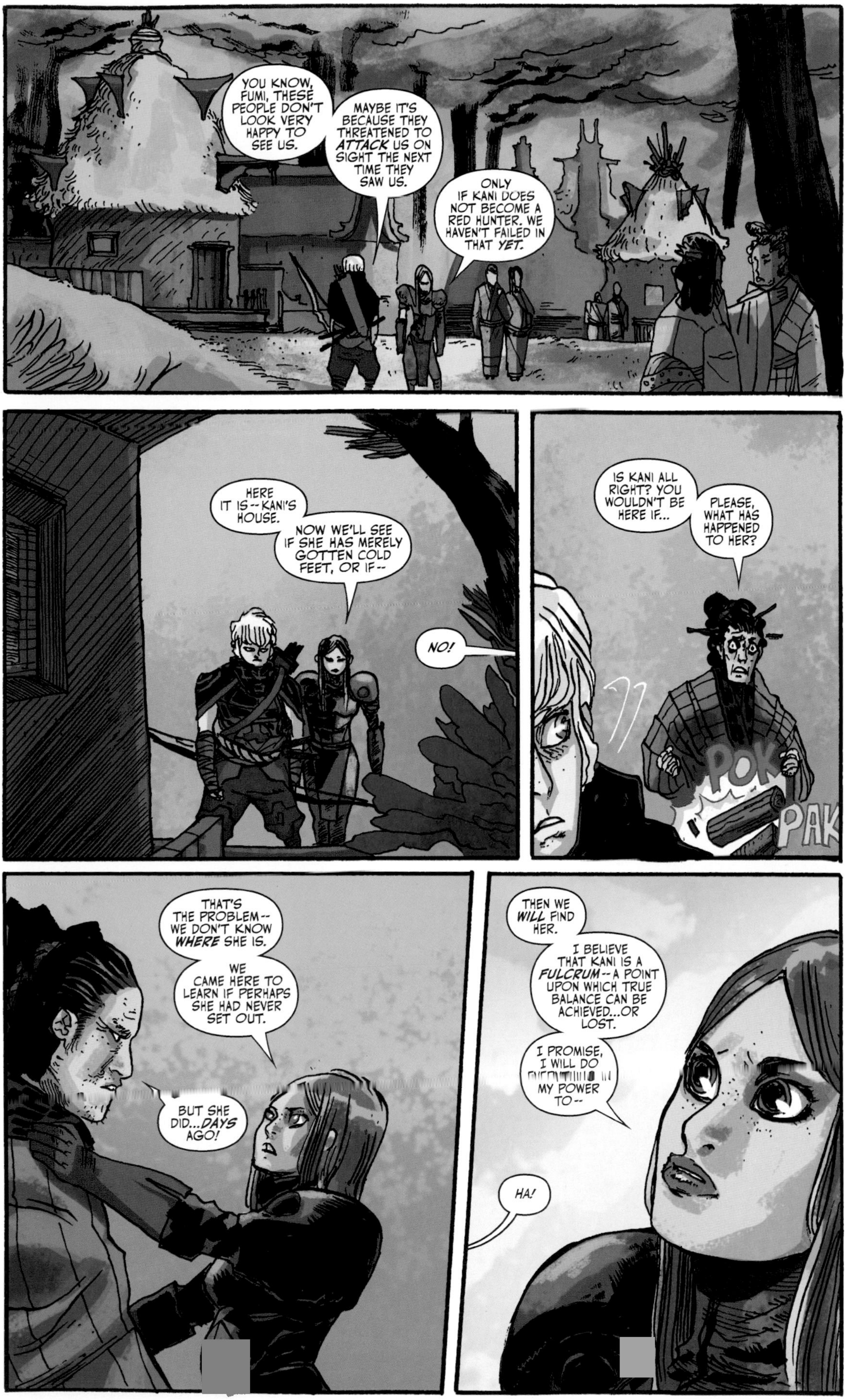

YOU KNOW, FUMI, THESE PEOPLE DON'T LOOK VERY HAPPY TO SEE US.
MAYBE IT'S BECAUSE THEY THREATENED TO ATTACK US ON SIGHT THE NEXT TIME THEY SAW US.
ONLY IF KANI DOES NOT BECOME A RED HUNTER. WE HAVEN'T FAILED IN THAT YET.
HERE IT IS--KANI'S HOUSE.
NOW WE'LL SEE IF SHE HAS MERELY GOTTEN COLD FEET, OR IF--
NO!
IS KANI ALL RIGHT? YOU WOULDN'T BE HERE IF...
PLEASE, WHAT HAS HAPPENED TO HER?
POK
PAK
THAT'S THE PROBLEM--WE DON'T KNOW WHERE SHE IS.
WE CAME HERE TO LEARN IF PERHAPS SHE HAD NEVER SET OUT.
BUT SHE DID...DAYS AGO!
THEN WE WILL FIND HER.
I BELIEVE THAT KANI IS A FULCRUM--A POINT UPON WHICH TRUE BALANCE CAN BE ACHIEVED...OR LOST.
I PROMISE, I WILL DO MY POWER TO--
HA!

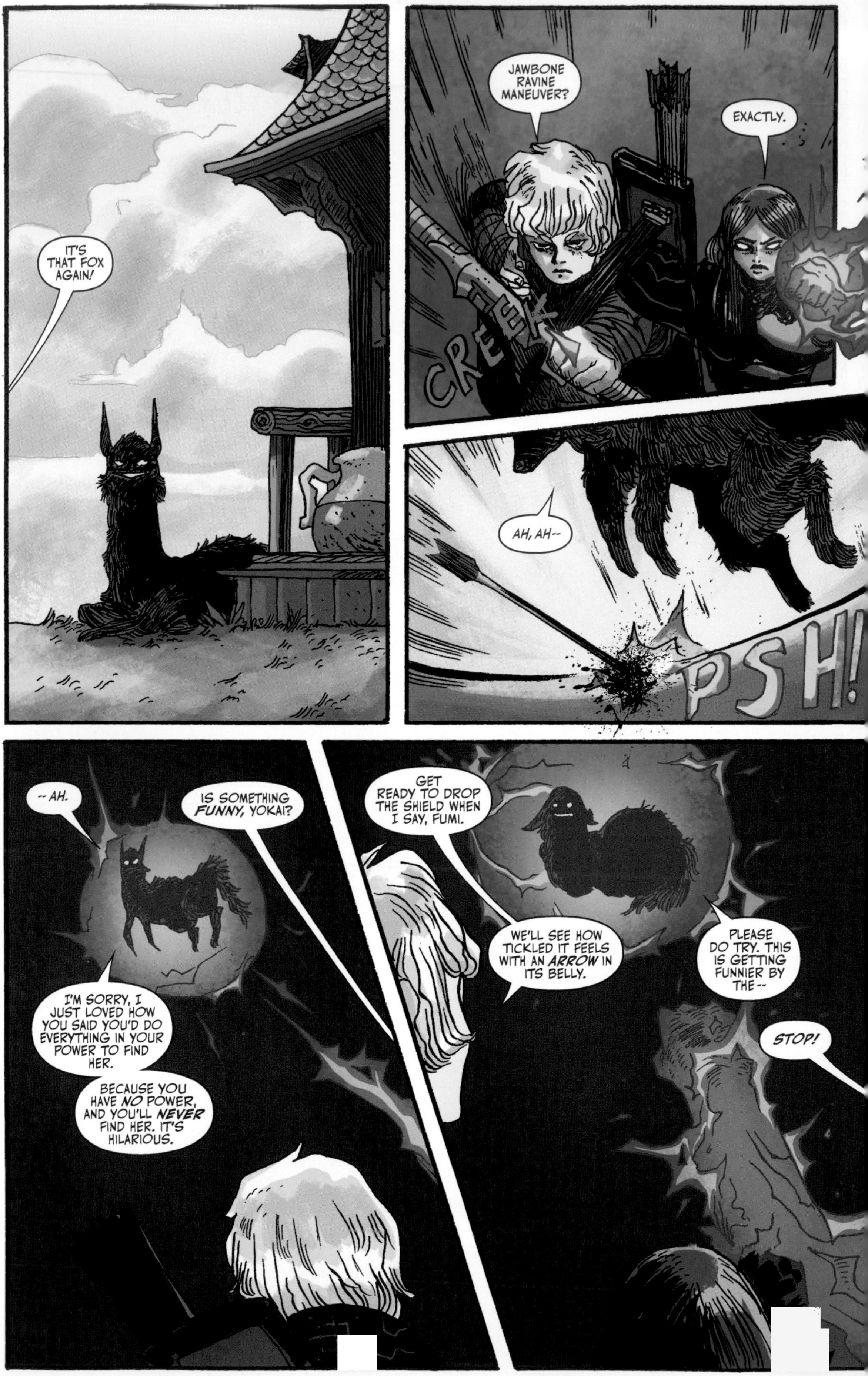
IT'S THAT FOX AGAIN!
JAWBONE RAVINE MANEUVER?
EXACTLY.
CREEEK
AH, AH--
PSH!
--AH.
IS SOMETHING FUNNY, YOKAI?
I'M SORRY, I JUST LOVED HOW YOU SAID YOU'D DO EVERYTHING IN YOUR POWER TO FIND HER.
BECAUSE YOU HAVE NO POWER, AND YOU'LL NEVER FIND HER. IT'S HILARIOUS.
GET READY TO DROP THE SHIELD WHEN I SAY, FUMI.
WE'LL SEE HOW TICKLED IT FEELS WITH AN ARROW IN ITS BELLY.
PLEASE DO TRY. THIS IS GETTING FUNNIER BY THE--
STOP!

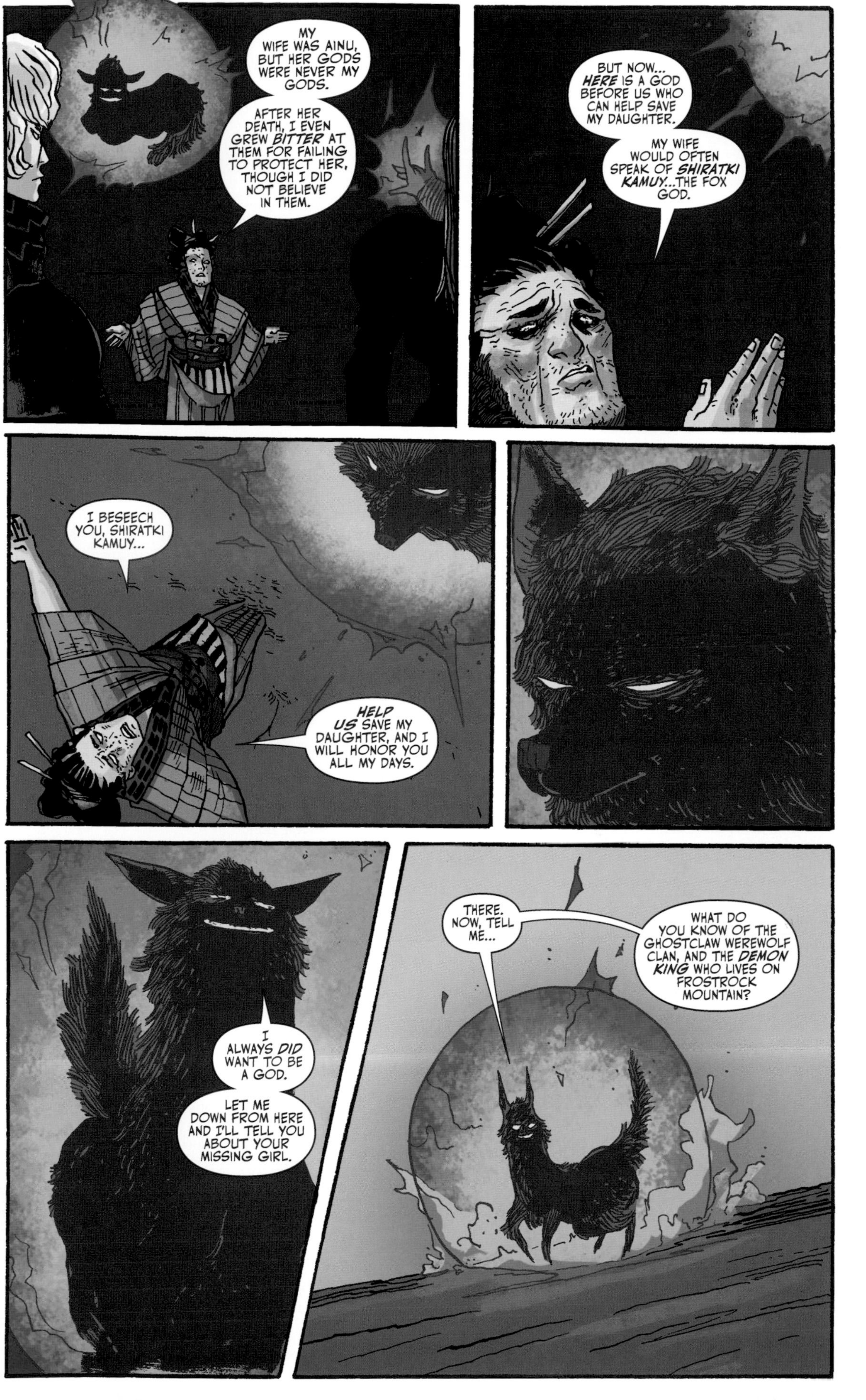
MY WIFE WAS AINU, BUT HER GODS WERE NEVER MY GODS.
AFTER HER DEATH, I EVEN GREW BITTER AT THEM FOR FAILING TO PROTECT HER, THOUGH I DID NOT BELIEVE IN THEM.
BUT NOW... HERE IS A GOD BEFORE US WHO CAN HELP SAVE MY DAUGHTER.
MY WIFE WOULD OFTEN SPEAK OF SHIRATKI KAMUY...THE FOX GOD.
I BESEECH YOU, SHIRATKI KAMUY...
HELP US SAVE MY DAUGHTER, AND I WILL HONOR YOU ALL MY DAYS.
I ALWAYS DID WANT TO BE A GOD.
LET ME DOWN FROM HERE AND I'LL TELL YOU ABOUT YOUR MISSING GIRL.
THERE. NOW, TELL ME...
WHAT DO YOU KNOW OF THE GHOSTCLAW WEREWOLF CLAN, AND THE DEMON KING WHO LIVES ON FROSTROCK MOUNTAIN?

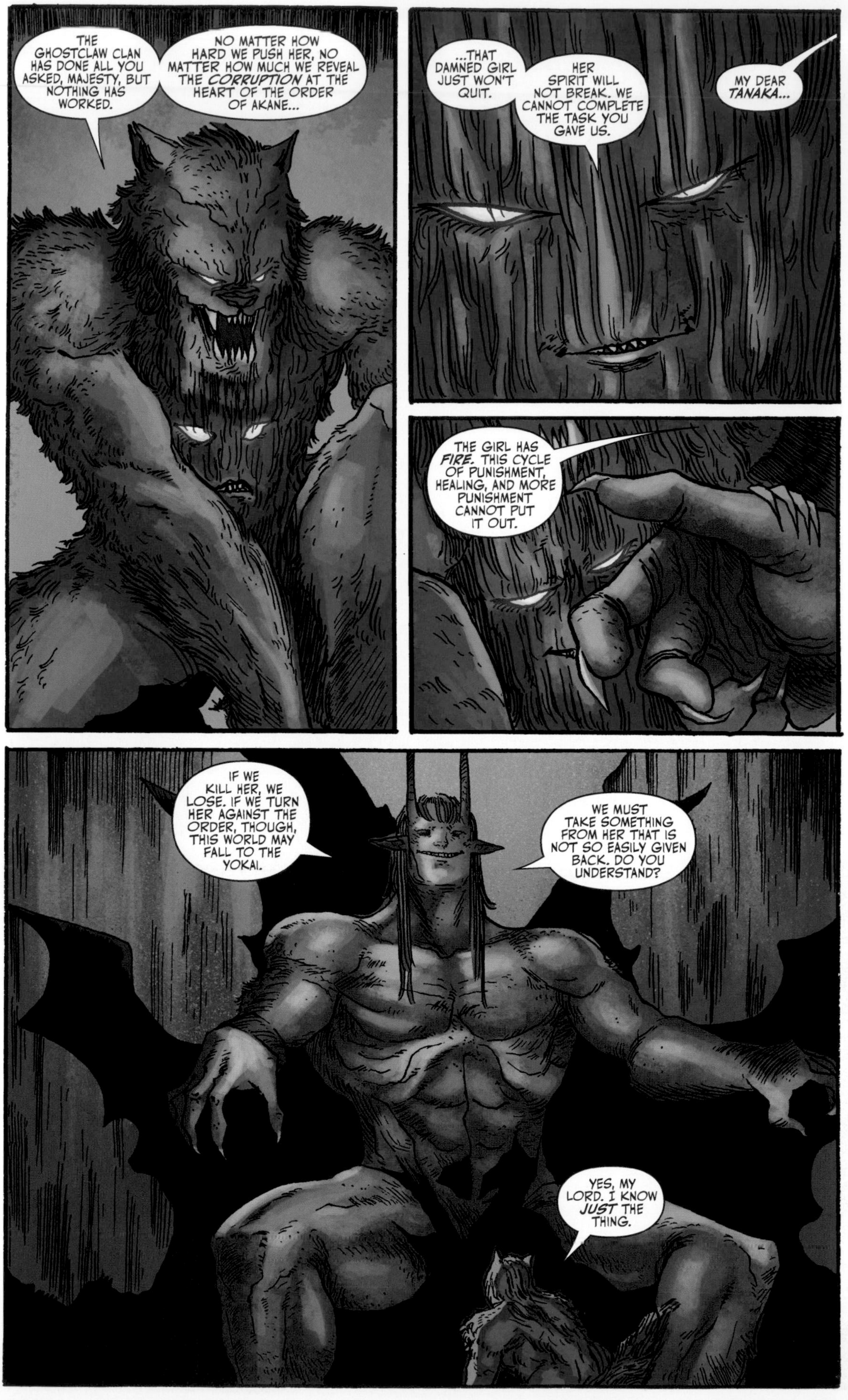
THE GHOSTCLAW CLAN HAS DONE ALL YOU ASKED, MAJESTY, BUT NOTHING HAS WORKED.
NO MATTER HOW HARD WE PUSH HER, NO MATTER HOW MUCH WE REVEAL THE CORRUPTION AT THE HEART OF THE ORDER OF AKANE...
...THAT DAMNED GIRL JUST WON'T QUIT.
HER SPIRIT WILL NOT BREAK. WE CANNOT COMPLETE THE TASK YOU GAVE US.
MY DEAR TANAKA...
THE GIRL HAS FIRE. THIS CYCLE OF PUNISHMENT, HEALING, AND MORE PUNISHMENT CANNOT PUT IT OUT.
IF WE KILL HER, WE LOSE. IF WE TURN HER AGAINST THE ORDER, THOUGH, THIS WORLD MAY FALL TO THE YOKAI.
WE MUST TAKE SOMETHING FROM HER THAT IS NOT SO EASILY GIVEN BACK. DO YOU UNDERSTAND?
YES, MY LORD. I KNOW JUST THE THING.

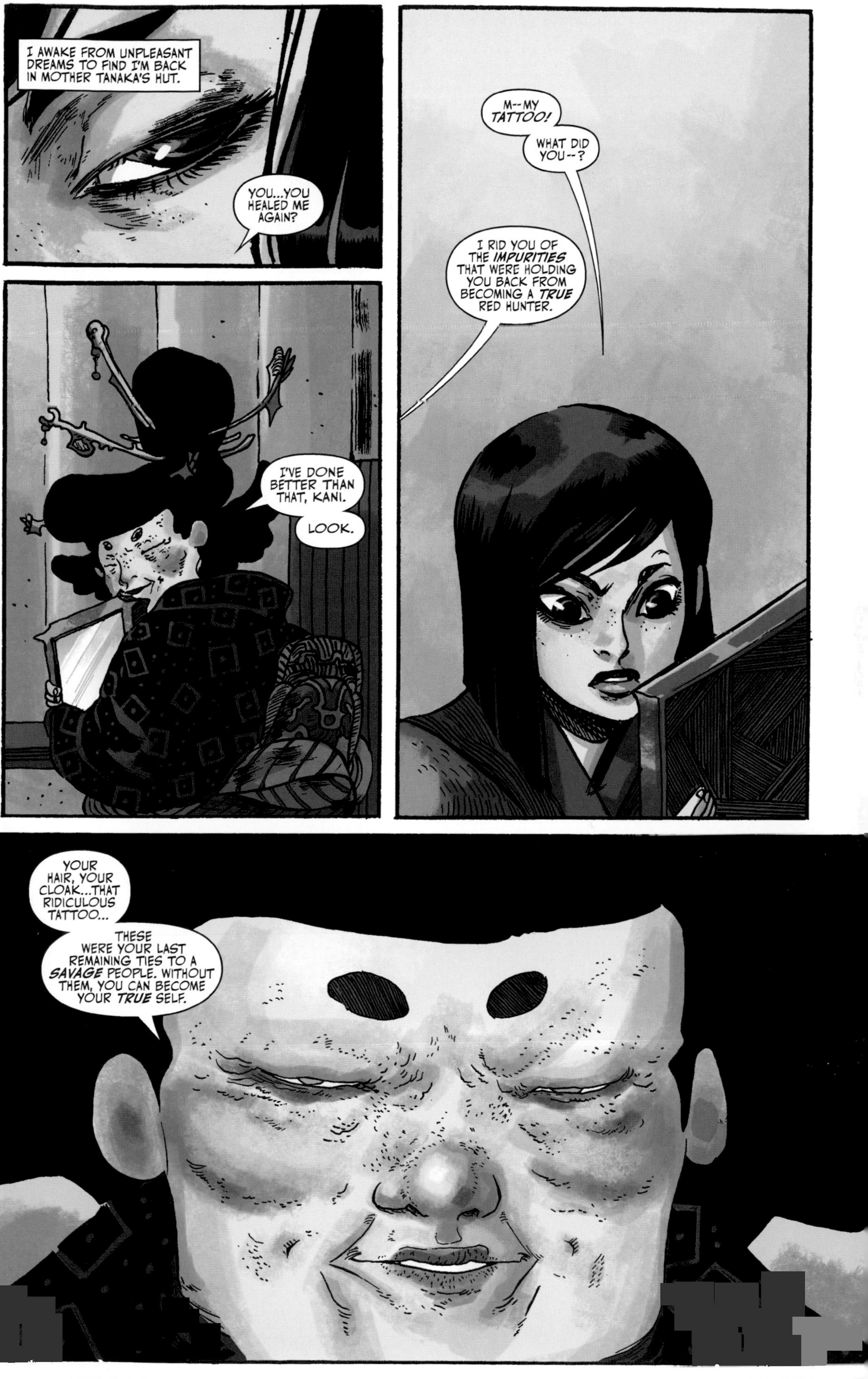
I AWAKE FROM UNPLEASANT DREAMS TO FIND I'M BACK IN MOTHER TANAKA'S HUT.
YOU...YOU HEALED ME AGAIN?
I'VE DONE BETTER THAN THAT, KANI.
LOOK.
M--MY TATTOO!
WHAT DID YOU--?
I RID YOU OF THE IMPURITIES THAT WERE HOLDING YOU BACK FROM BECOMING A TRUE RED HUNTER.
YOUR HAIR, YOUR CLOAK...THAT RIDICULOUS TATTOO...
THESE WERE YOUR LAST REMAINING TIES TO A SAVAGE PEOPLE. WITHOUT THEM, YOU CAN BECOME YOUR TRUE SELF.

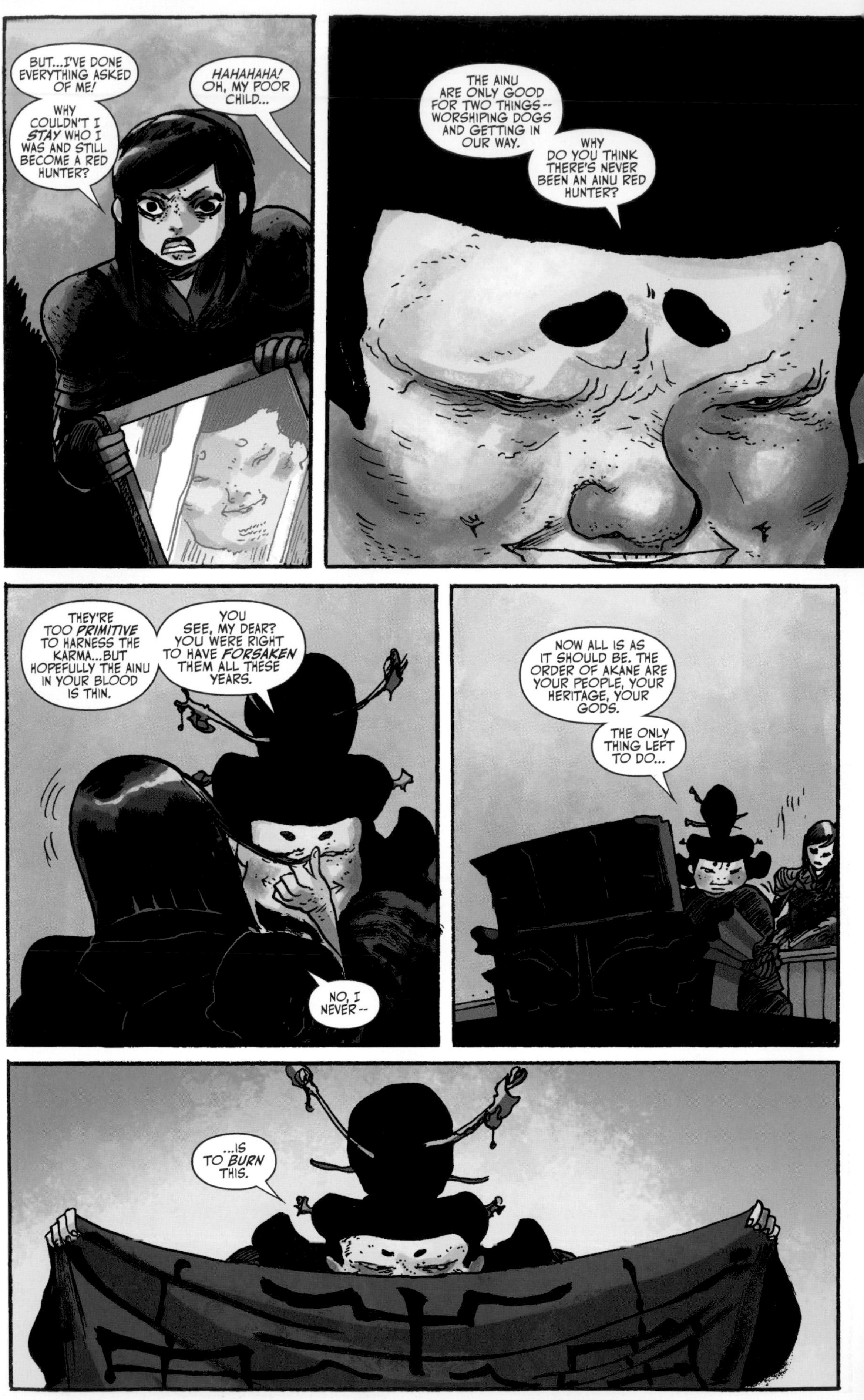
BUT...I'VE DONE EVERYTHING ASKED OF ME!
WHY COULDN'T I STAY WHO I WAS AND STILL BECOME A RED HUNTER?
HAHAHAHA! OH, MY POOR CHILD...
THE AINU ARE ONLY GOOD FOR TWO THINGS--WORSHIPING DOGS AND GETTING IN OUR WAY.
WHY DO YOU THINK THERE'S NEVER BEEN AN AINU RED HUNTER?
THEY'RE TOO PRIMITIVE TO HARNESS THE KARMA...BUT HOPEFULLY THE AINU IN YOUR BLOOD IS THIN.
YOU SEE, MY DEAR? YOU WERE RIGHT TO HAVE FORSAKEN THEM ALL THESE YEARS.
NO, I NEVER--
NOW ALL IS AS IT SHOULD BE. THE ORDER OF AKANE ARE YOUR PEOPLE, YOUR HERITAGE, YOUR GODS.
THE ONLY THING LEFT TO DO...
...IS TO BURN THIS.

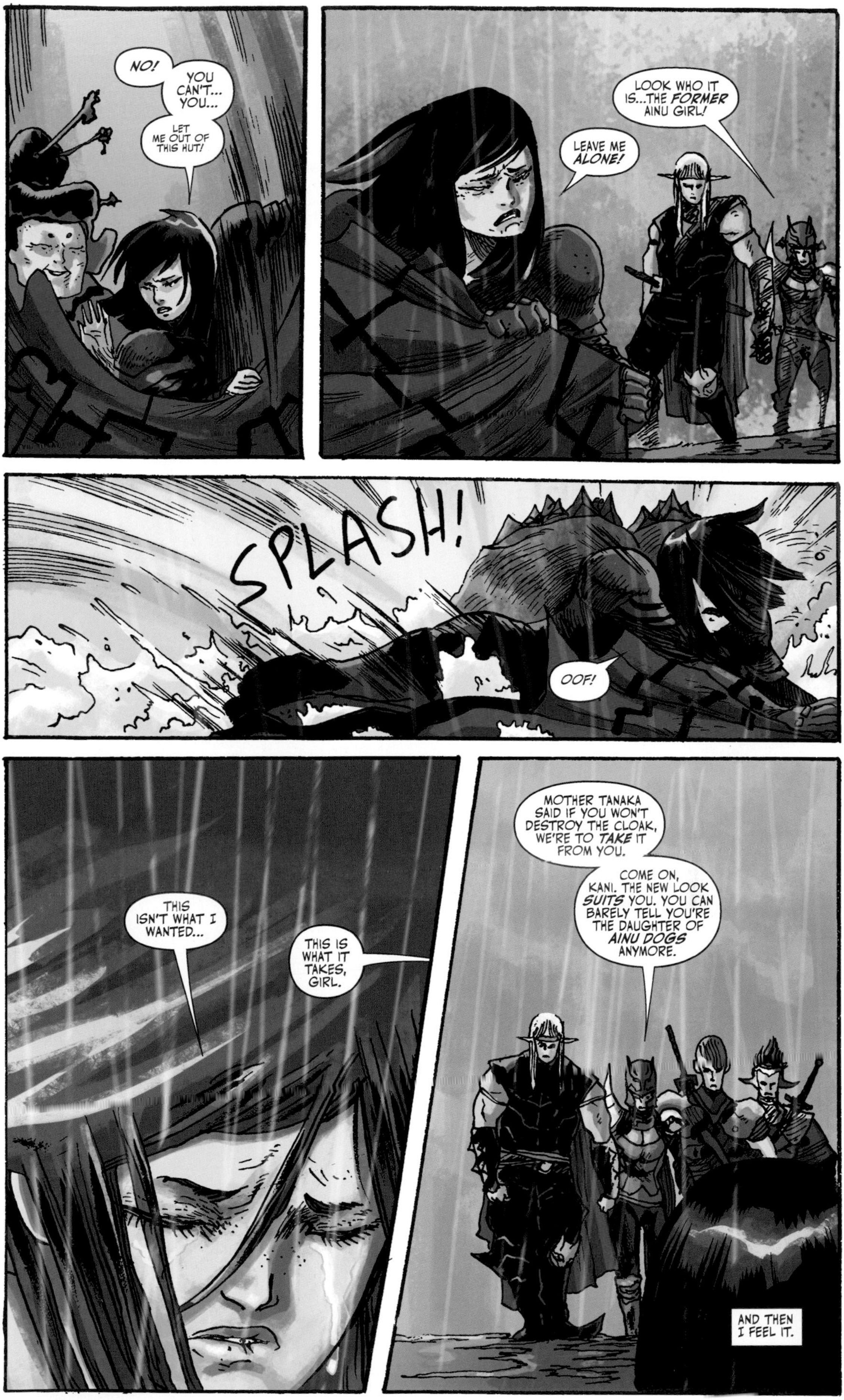
NO!
YOU CAN'T... YOU...
LET ME OUT OF THIS HUT!
LOOK WHO IT IS...THE FORMER AINU GIRL!
LEAVE ME ALONE!
SPLASH!
OOF!
THIS ISN'T WHAT I WANTED...
THIS IS WHAT IT TAKES, GIRL.
MOTHER TANAKA SAID IF YOU WON'T DESTROY THE CLOAK, WE'RE TO TAKE IT FROM YOU.
COME ON, KANI. THE NEW LOOK SUITS YOU. YOU CAN BARELY TELL YOU'RE THE DAUGHTER OF AINU DOGS ANYMORE.
AND THEN I FEEL IT.

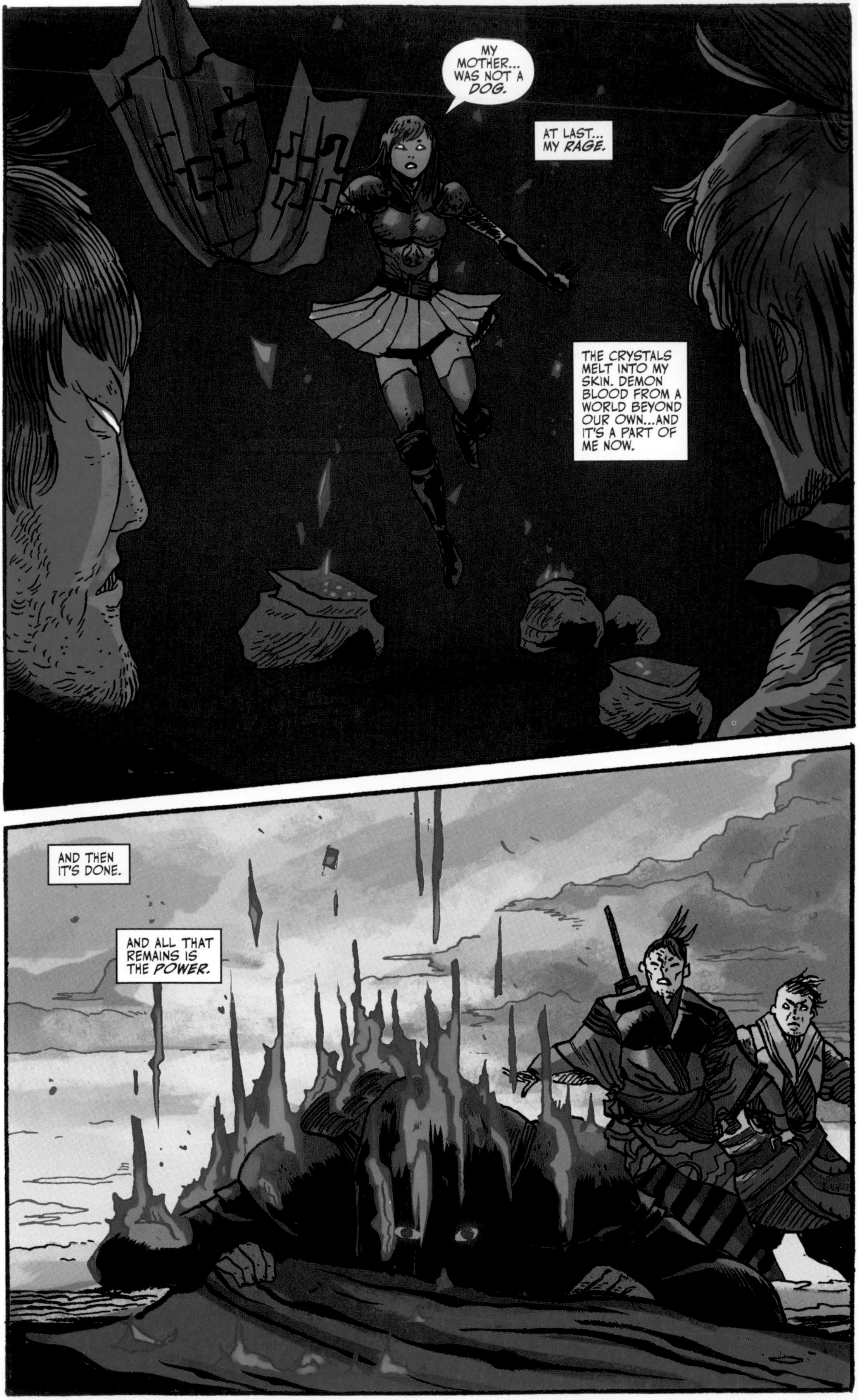
MY MOTHER... WAS NOT A DOG.
AT LAST... MY RAGE.
THE CRYSTALS MELT INTO MY SKIN. DEMON BLOOD FROM A WORLD BEYOND OUR OWN...AND IT'S A PART OF ME NOW.
AND THEN IT'S DONE.
AND ALL THAT REMAINS IS THE POWER.

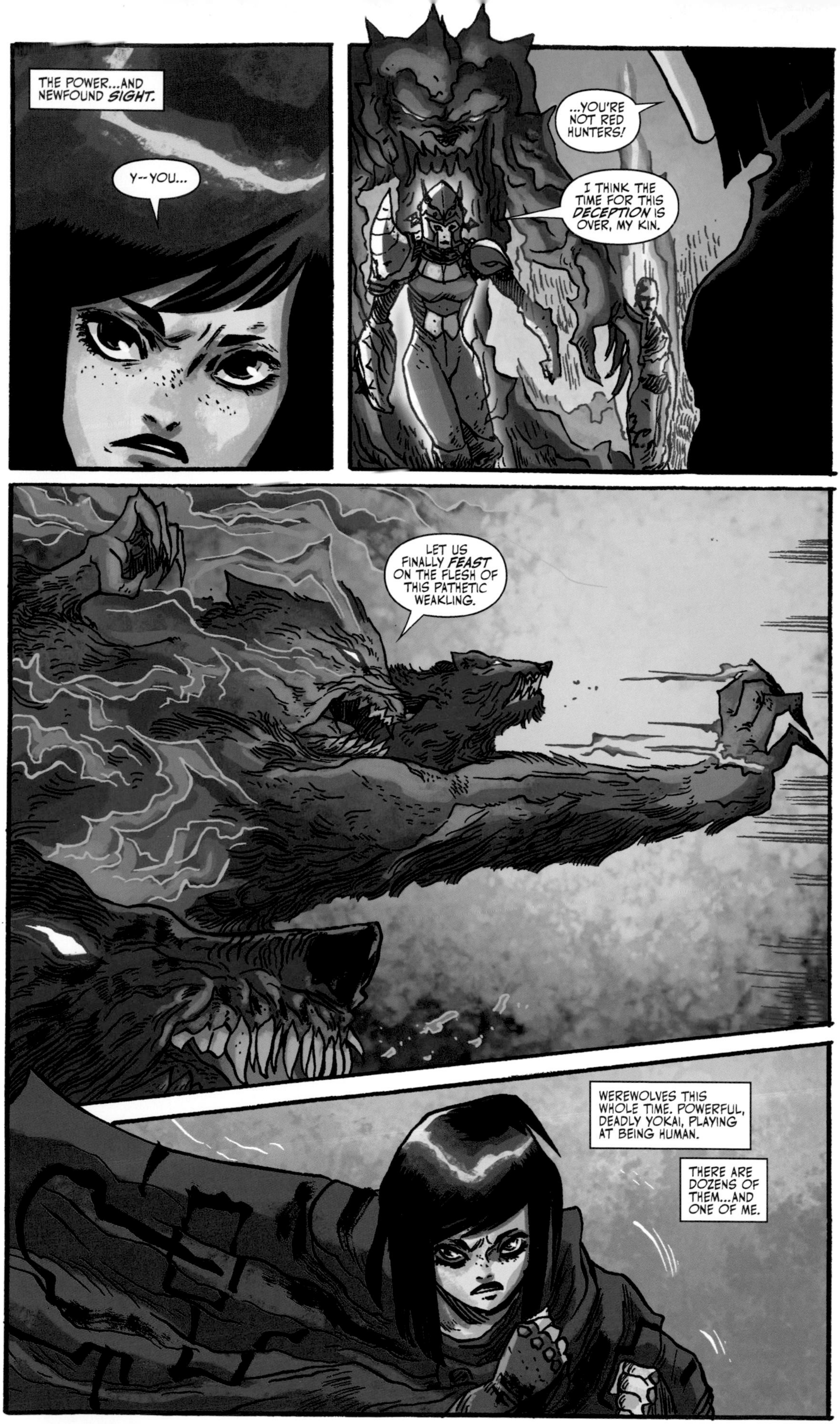
THE POWER...AND NEWFOUND *SIGHT*.
Y--YOU...
...YOU'RE NOT RED HUNTERS!
I THINK THE TIME FOR THIS *DECEPTION* IS OVER, MY KIN.
LET US FINALLY *FEAST* ON THE FLESH OF THIS PATHETIC WEAKLING.
WEREWOLVES THIS WHOLE TIME. POWERFUL, DEADLY YOKAI, PLAYING AT BEING HUMAN.
THERE ARE DOZENS OF THEM...AND ONE OF ME.

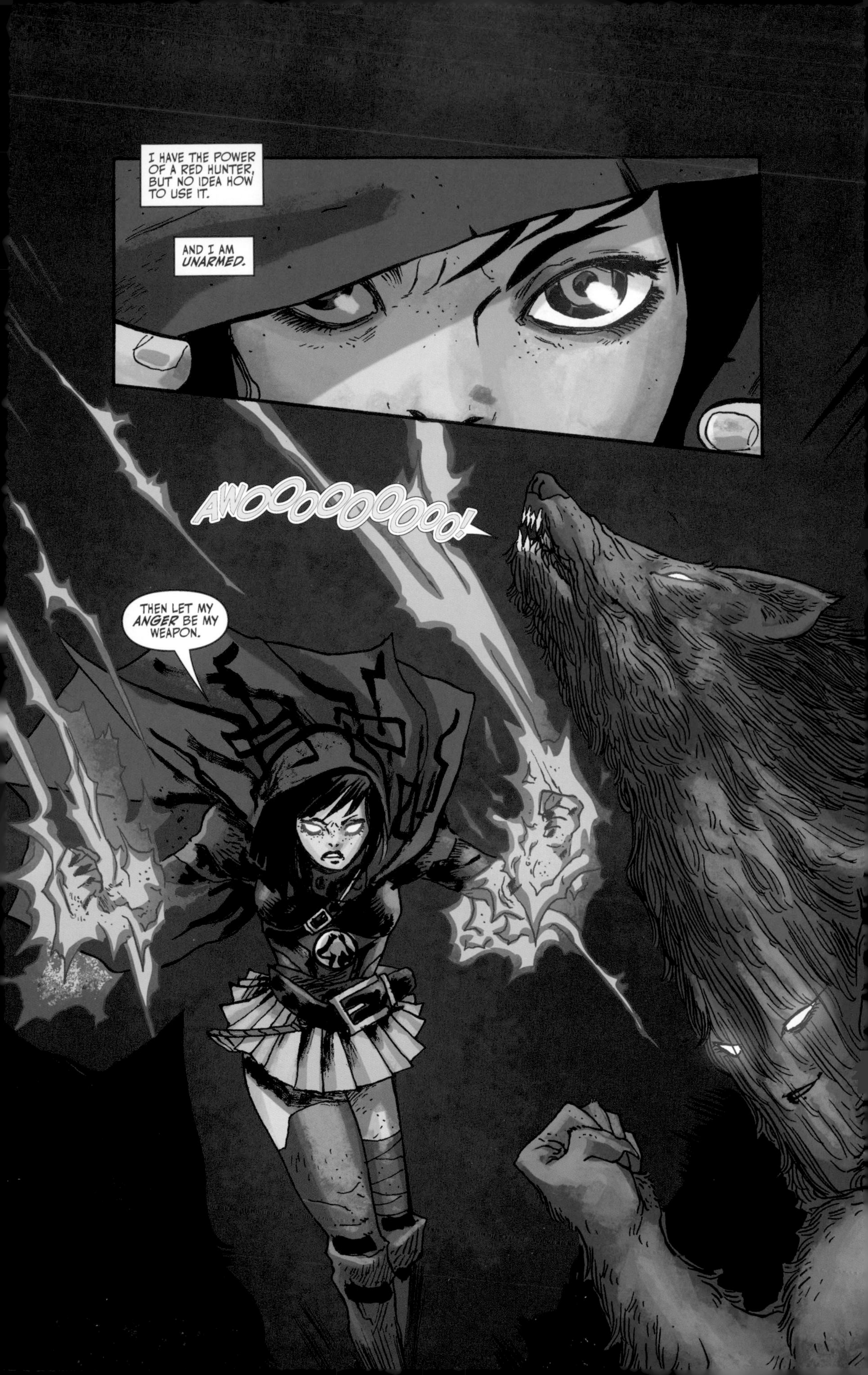
I HAVE THE POWER OF A RED HUNTER, BUT NO IDEA HOW TO USE IT.
AND I AM *UNARMED.*
AWOOOOOOOOOOO!
THEN LET MY *ANGER* BE MY WEAPON.

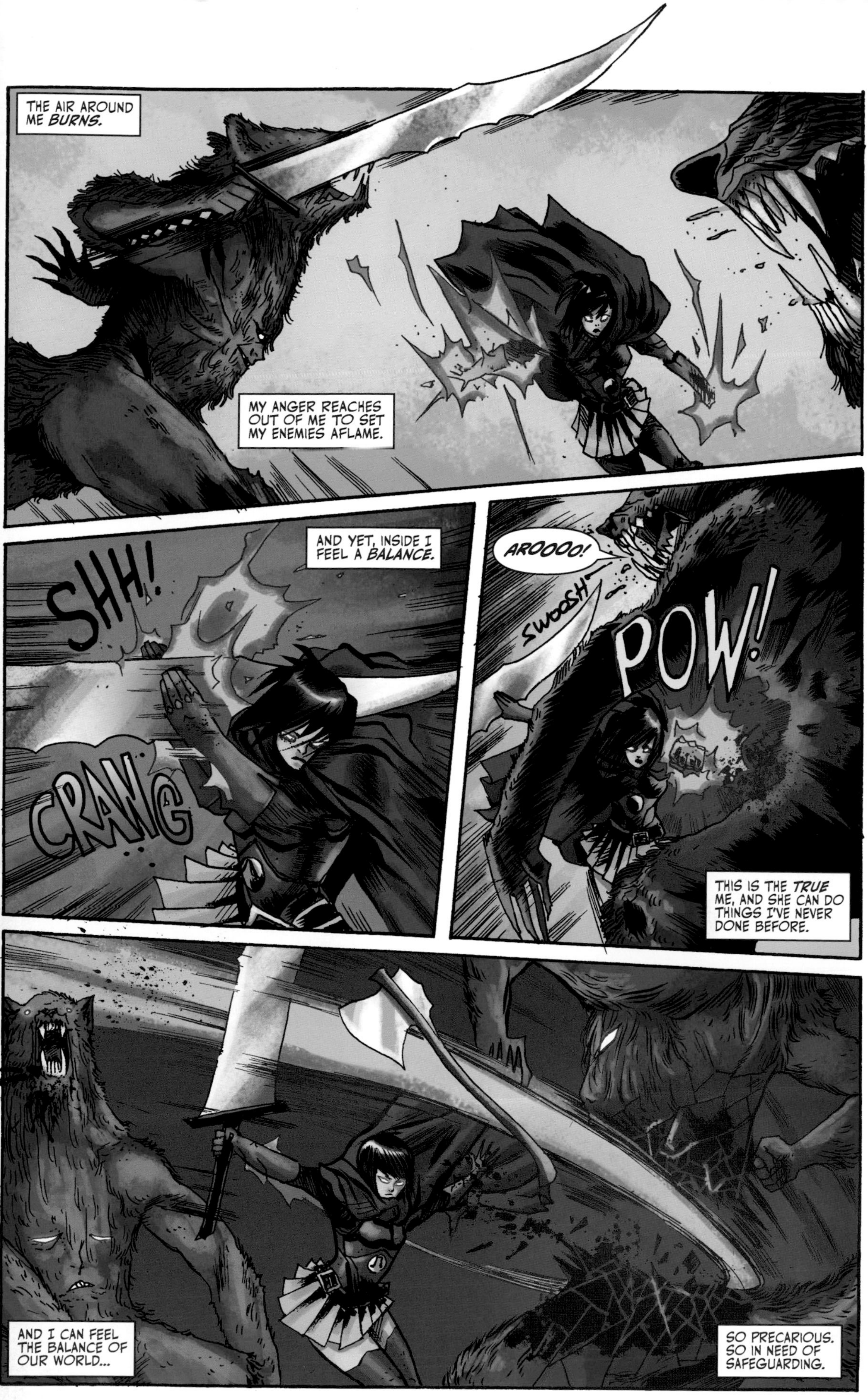
THE AIR AROUND ME BURNS.
MY ANGER REACHES OUT OF ME TO SET MY ENEMIES AFLAME.
AND YET, INSIDE I FEEL A BALANCE.
SHH!
CRANG
AROOOO!
SWOOSH
POW!
THIS IS THE TRUE ME, AND SHE CAN DO THINGS I'VE NEVER DONE BEFORE.
AND I CAN FEEL THE BALANCE OF OUR WORLD...
SO PRECARIOUS. SO IN NEED OF SAFEGUARDING.

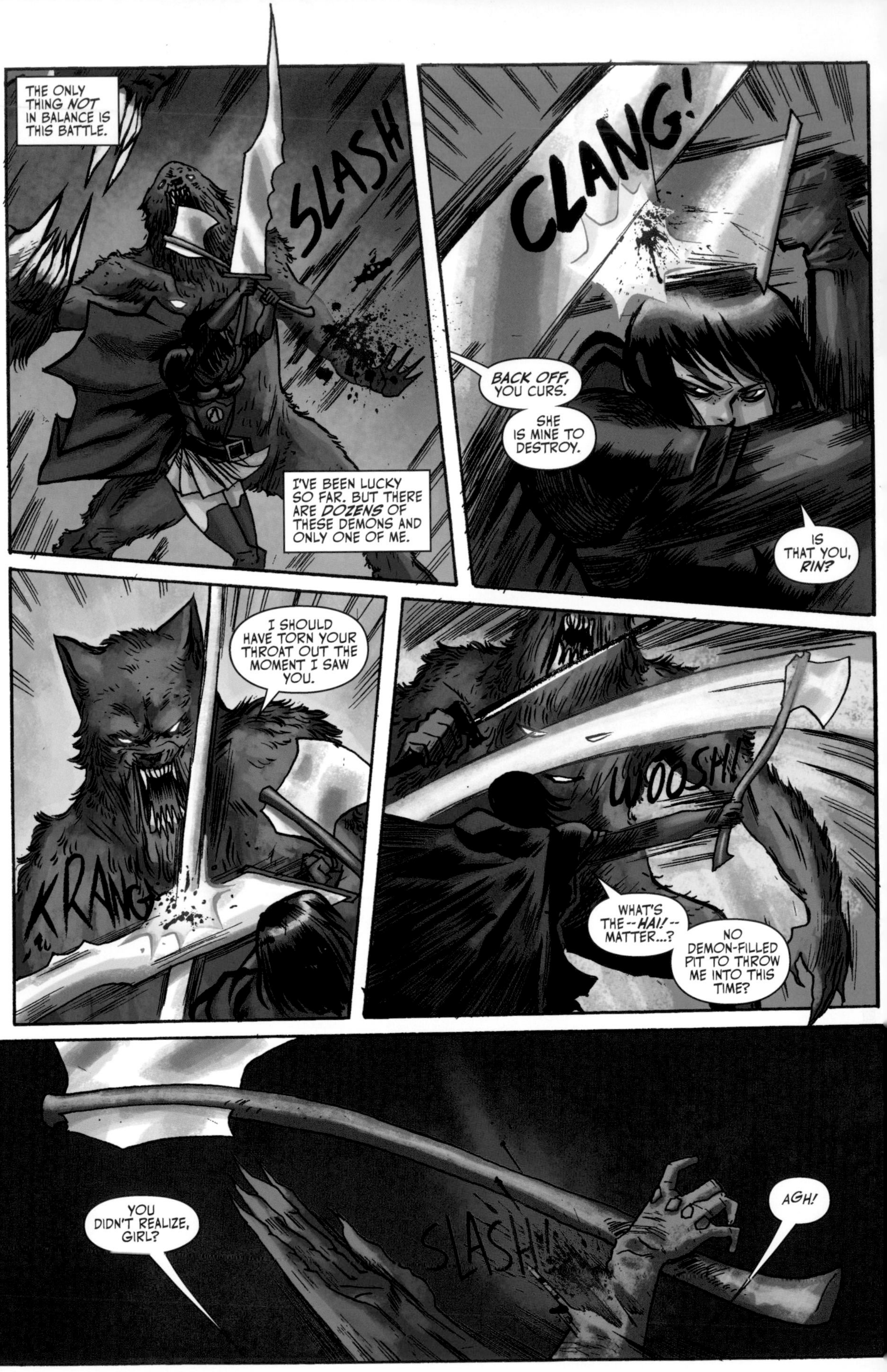

THE ONLY THING *NOT* IN BALANCE IS THIS BATTLE.
SLASH
I'VE BEEN LUCKY SO FAR. BUT THERE ARE *DOZENS* OF THESE DEMONS AND ONLY ONE OF ME.
CLANG!
BACK OFF, YOU CURS.
SHE IS MINE TO DESTROY.
IS THAT YOU, *RIN?*
I SHOULD HAVE TORN YOUR THROAT OUT THE MOMENT I SAW YOU.
KRANG
WOOSH!
WHAT'S THE --*HAI!*-- MATTER...?
NO DEMON-FILLED PIT TO THROW ME INTO THIS TIME?
YOU DIDN'T REALIZE, GIRL?
SLASH!
AGH!

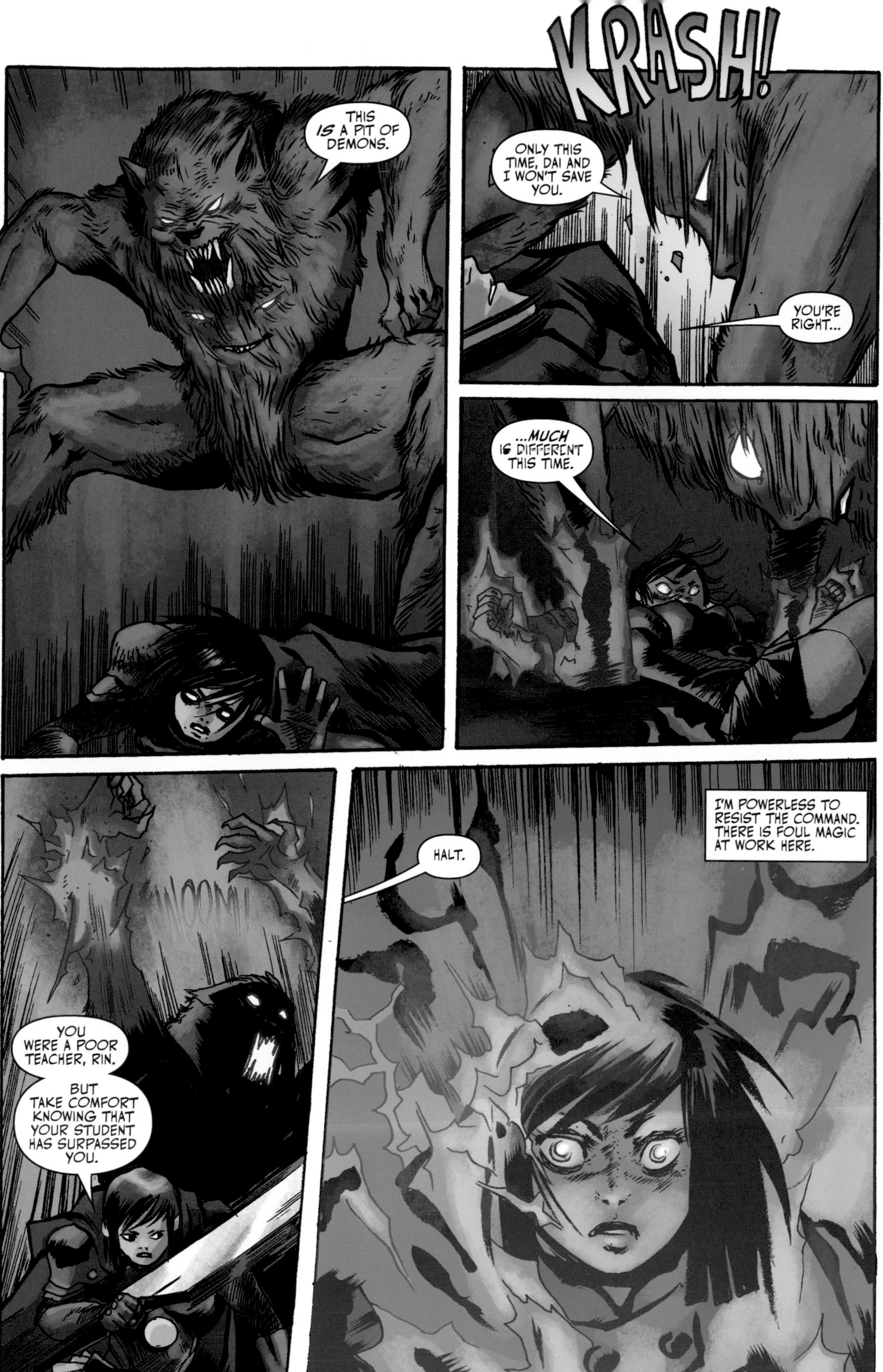
THIS IS A PIT OF DEMONS.
KRASH!
ONLY THIS TIME, DAI AND I WON'T SAVE YOU.
YOU'RE RIGHT...
...MUCH IS DIFFERENT THIS TIME.
WOOM!
YOU WERE A POOR TEACHER, RIN.
BUT TAKE COMFORT KNOWING THAT YOUR STUDENT HAS SURPASSED YOU.
HALT.
I'M POWERLESS TO RESIST THE COMMAND. THERE IS FOUL MAGIC AT WORK HERE.

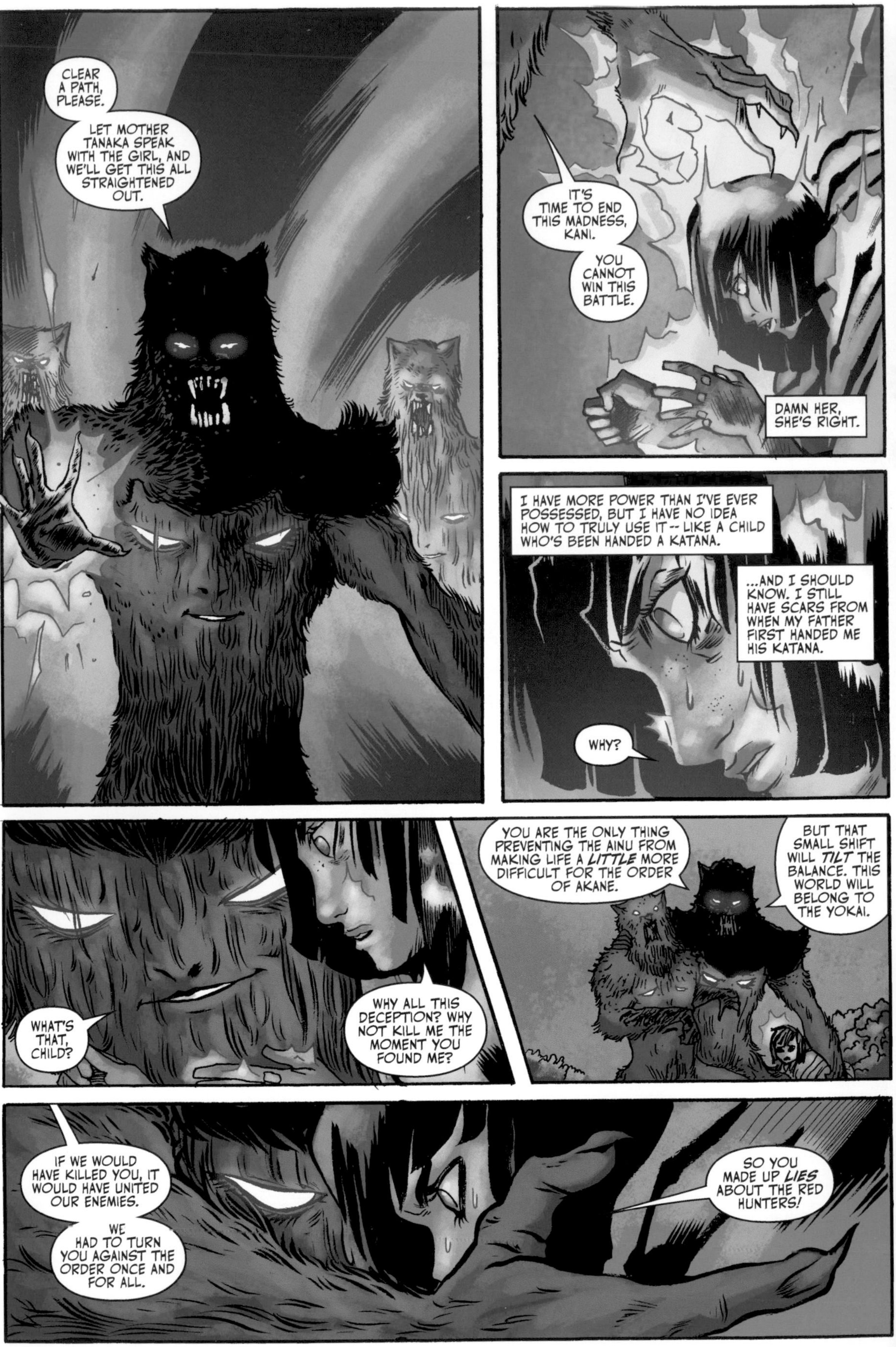
CLEAR A PATH, PLEASE.
LET MOTHER TANAKA SPEAK WITH THE GIRL, AND WE'LL GET THIS ALL STRAIGHTENED OUT.
IT'S TIME TO END THIS MADNESS, KANI.
YOU CANNOT WIN THIS BATTLE.
DAMN HER, SHE'S RIGHT.
I HAVE MORE POWER THAN I'VE EVER POSSESSED, BUT I HAVE NO IDEA HOW TO TRULY USE IT -- LIKE A CHILD WHO'S BEEN HANDED A KATANA.
...AND I SHOULD KNOW. I STILL HAVE SCARS FROM WHEN MY FATHER FIRST HANDED ME HIS KATANA.
WHY?
WHAT'S THAT, CHILD?
WHY ALL THIS DECEPTION? WHY NOT KILL ME THE MOMENT YOU FOUND ME?
YOU ARE THE ONLY THING PREVENTING THE AINU FROM MAKING LIFE A *LITTLE* MORE DIFFICULT FOR THE ORDER OF AKANE.
BUT THAT SMALL SHIFT WILL *TILT* THE BALANCE. THIS WORLD WILL BELONG TO THE YOKAI.
IF WE WOULD HAVE KILLED YOU, IT WOULD HAVE UNITED OUR ENEMIES.
WE HAD TO TURN YOU AGAINST THE ORDER ONCE AND FOR ALL.
SO YOU MADE UP *LIES* ABOUT THE RED HUNTERS!

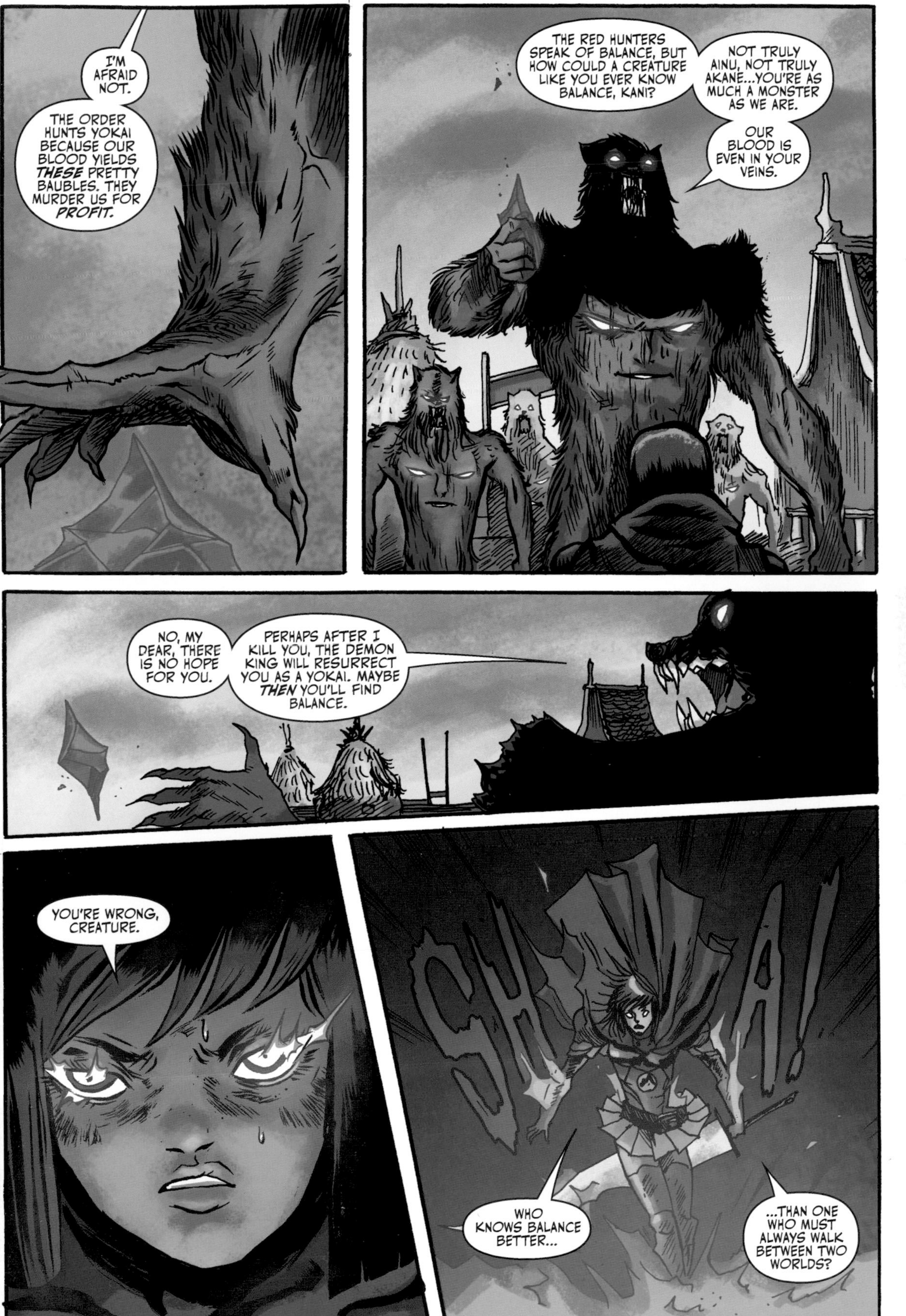
I'M AFRAID NOT.
THE ORDER HUNTS YOKAI BECAUSE OUR BLOOD YIELDS *THESE* PRETTY BAUBLES. THEY MURDER US FOR *PROFIT.*
THE RED HUNTERS SPEAK OF BALANCE, BUT HOW COULD A CREATURE LIKE YOU EVER KNOW BALANCE, KANI?
NOT TRULY AINU, NOT TRULY AKANE...YOU'RE AS MUCH A MONSTER AS WE ARE.
OUR BLOOD IS EVEN IN YOUR VEINS.
NO, MY DEAR, THERE IS NO HOPE FOR YOU.
PERHAPS AFTER I KILL YOU, THE DEMON KING WILL RESURRECT YOU AS A YOKAI. MAYBE *THEN* YOU'LL FIND BALANCE.
YOU'RE WRONG, CREATURE.
SHA!
WHO KNOWS BALANCE BETTER...
...THAN ONE WHO MUST ALWAYS WALK BETWEEN TWO WORLDS?

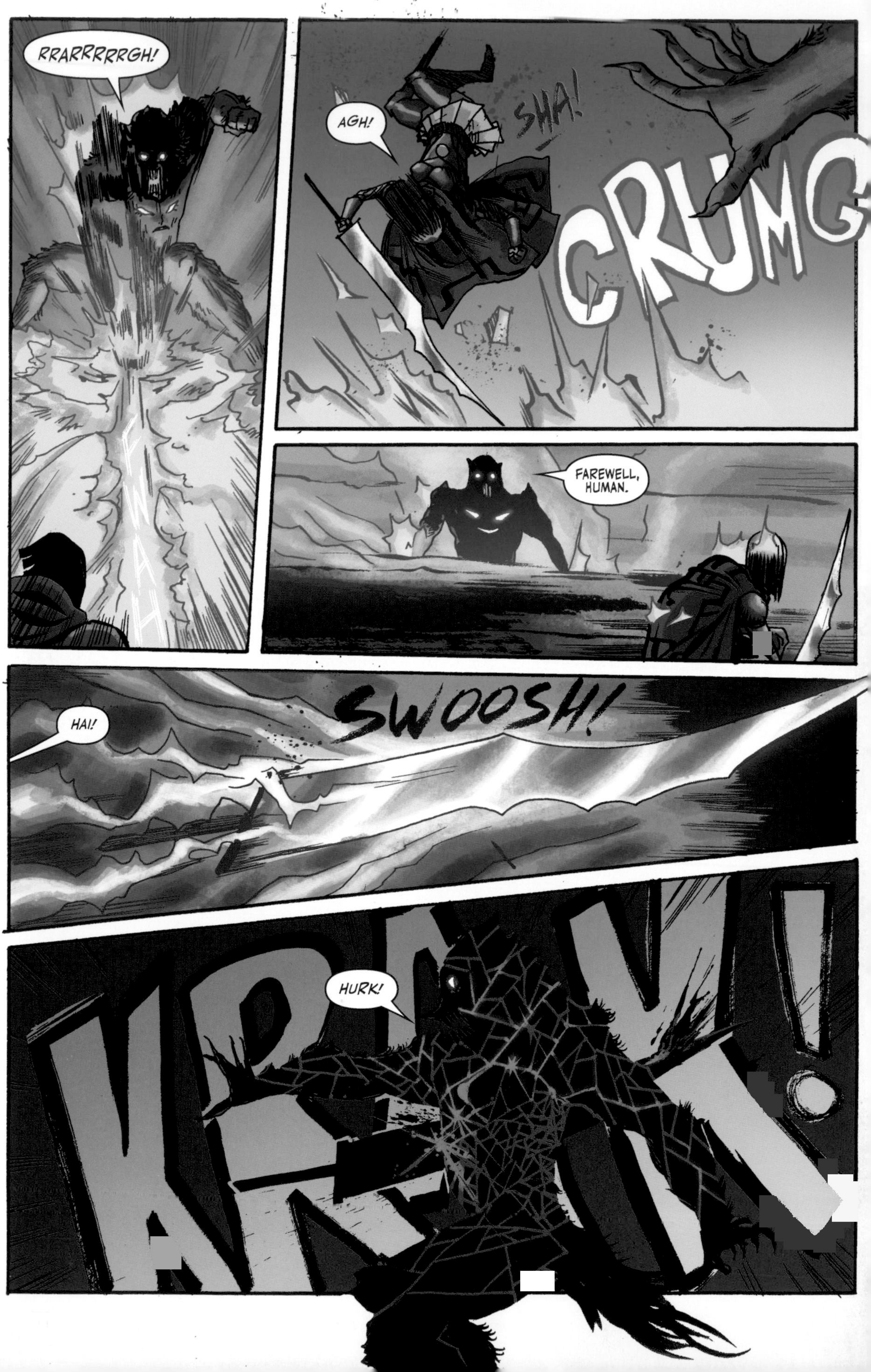
RRARRRRRGH!
AGH!
SHA!
CRUMG
FAREWELL, HUMAN.
HAI!
SWOOSH!
HURK!

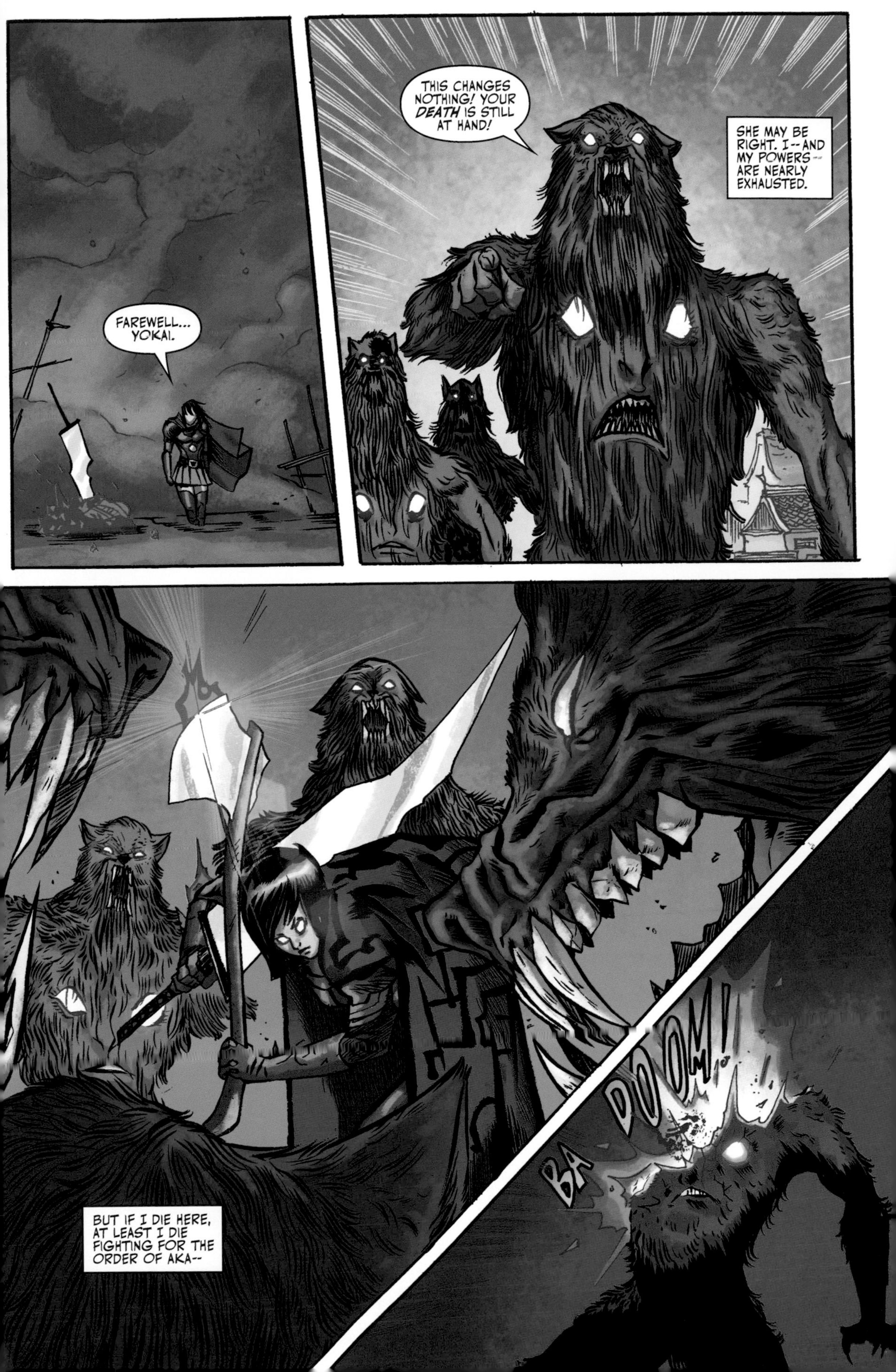
FAREWELL... YOKAI.
THIS CHANGES NOTHING! YOUR DEATH IS STILL AT HAND!
SHE MAY BE RIGHT. I--AND MY POWERS--ARE NEARLY EXHAUSTED.
BUT IF I DIE HERE, AT LEAST I DIE FIGHTING FOR THE ORDER OF AKA--
BA DOOOM!

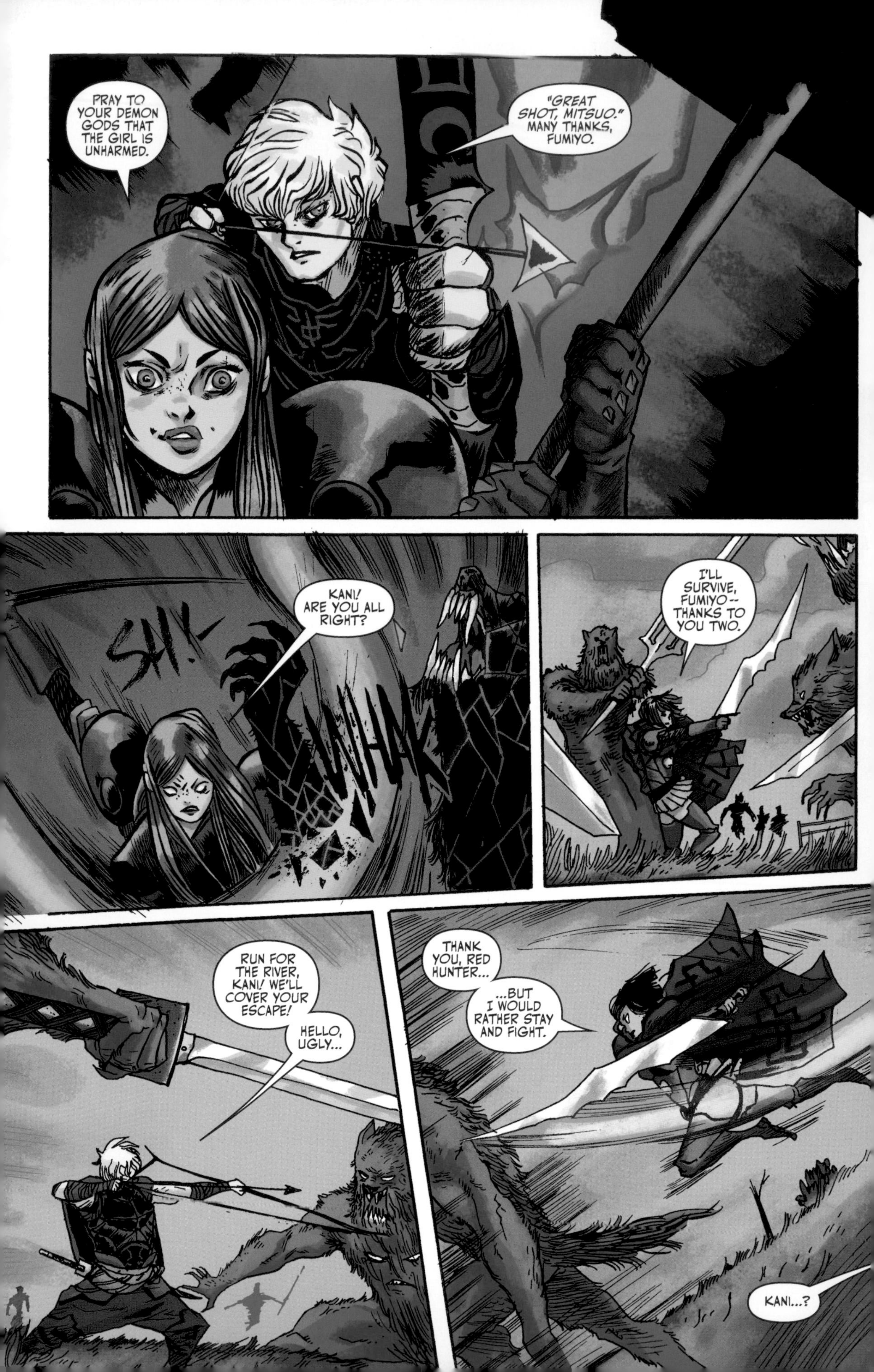
PRAY TO YOUR DEMON GODS THAT THE GIRL IS UNHARMED.
"GREAT SHOT, MITSUO." MANY THANKS, FUMIYO.
SHK-
KANI! ARE YOU ALL RIGHT?
WHHAK
I'LL SURVIVE, FUMIYO-- THANKS TO YOU TWO.
RUN FOR THE RIVER, KANI! WE'LL COVER YOUR ESCAPE!
HELLO, UGLY...
THANK YOU, RED HUNTER...
...BUT I WOULD RATHER STAY AND FIGHT.
KANI...?

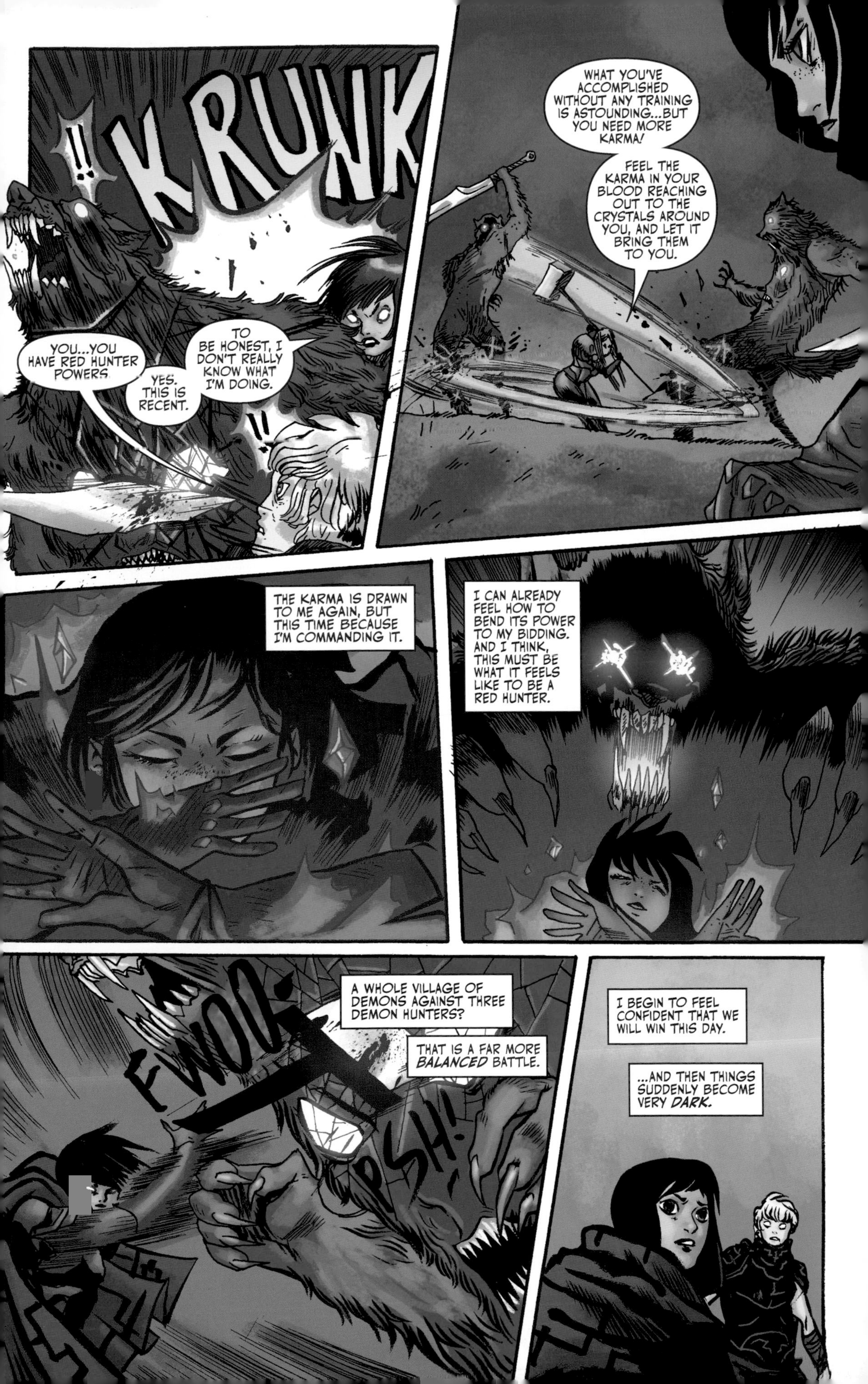
!!
KRUNK
YOU...YOU HAVE RED HUNTER POWERS.
YES. THIS IS RECENT.
TO BE HONEST, I DON'T REALLY KNOW WHAT I'M DOING.
!!
WHAT YOU'VE ACCOMPLISHED WITHOUT ANY TRAINING IS ASTOUNDING...BUT YOU NEED MORE KARMA!
FEEL THE KARMA IN YOUR BLOOD REACHING OUT TO THE CRYSTALS AROUND YOU, AND LET IT BRING THEM TO YOU.
THE KARMA IS DRAWN TO ME AGAIN, BUT THIS TIME BECAUSE I'M COMMANDING IT.
I CAN ALREADY FEEL HOW TO BEND ITS POWER TO MY BIDDING. AND I THINK, THIS MUST BE WHAT IT FEELS LIKE TO BE A RED HUNTER.
A WHOLE VILLAGE OF DEMONS AGAINST THREE DEMON HUNTERS?
THAT IS A FAR MORE *BALANCED* BATTLE.
FWOO
PSH!
I BEGIN TO FEEL CONFIDENT THAT WE WILL WIN THIS DAY.
...AND THEN THINGS SUDDENLY BECOME VERY *DARK.*

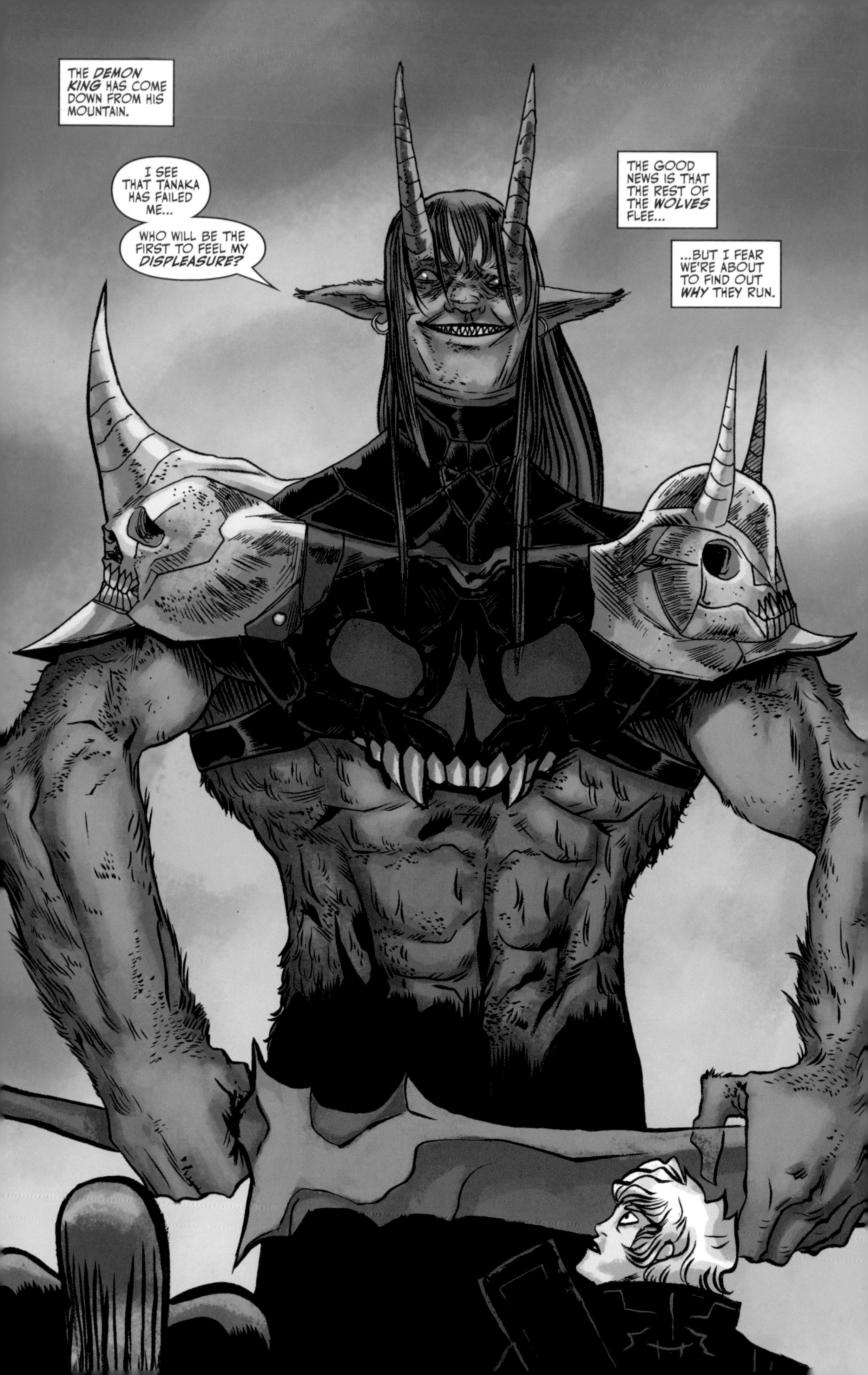
THE *DEMON KING* HAS COME DOWN FROM HIS MOUNTAIN.
I SEE THAT TANAKA HAS FAILED ME...
WHO WILL BE THE FIRST TO FEEL MY *DISPLEASURE?*
THE GOOD NEWS IS THAT THE REST OF THE *WOLVES* FLEE...
...BUT I FEAR WE'RE ABOUT TO FIND OUT *WHY* THEY RUN.

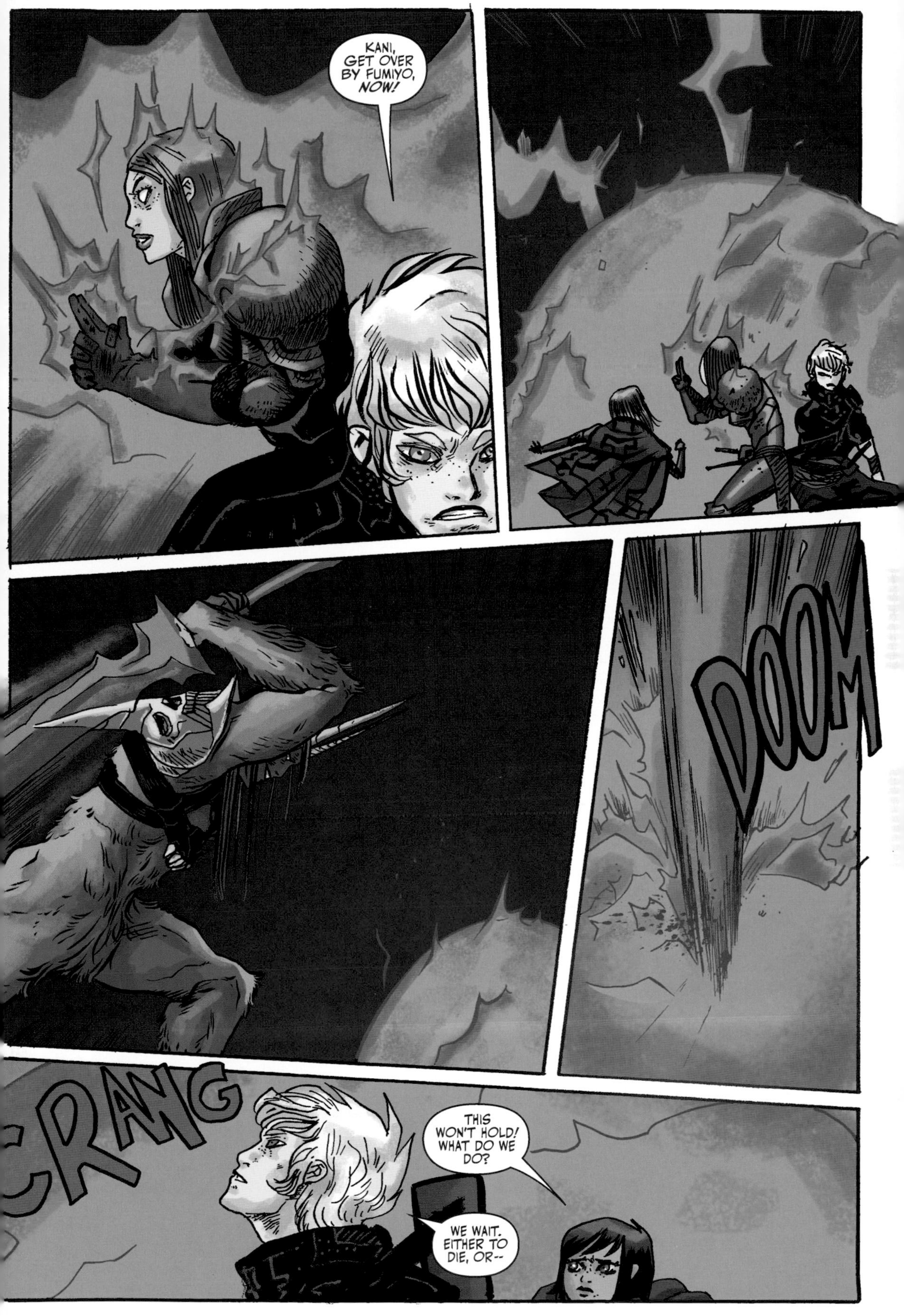
KANI, GET OVER BY FUMIYO, *NOW!*
DOOM
CRANG
THIS WON'T HOLD! WHAT DO WE DO?
WE WAIT. EITHER TO DIE, OR--

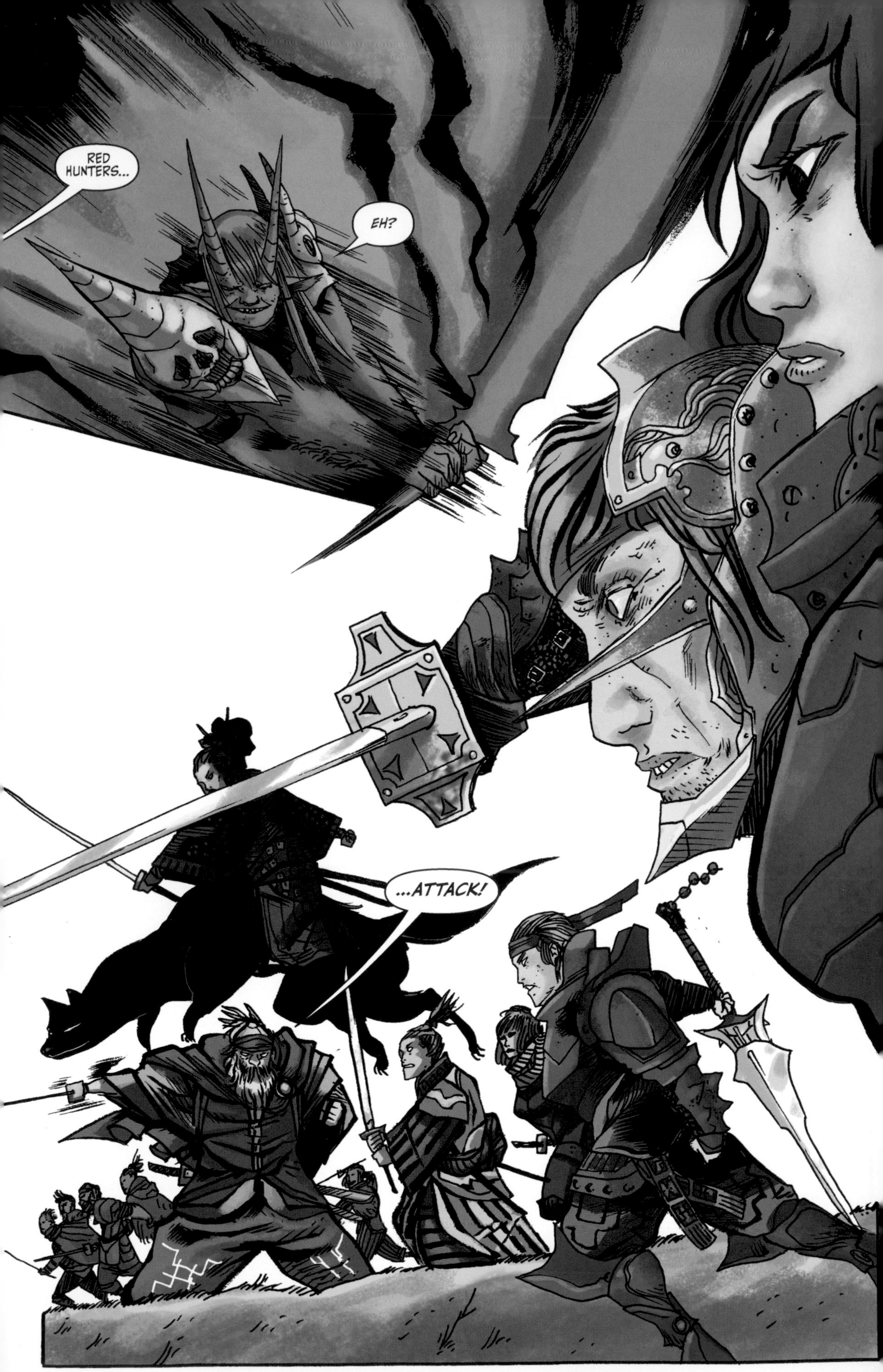
RED HUNTERS...
EH?
...ATTACK!

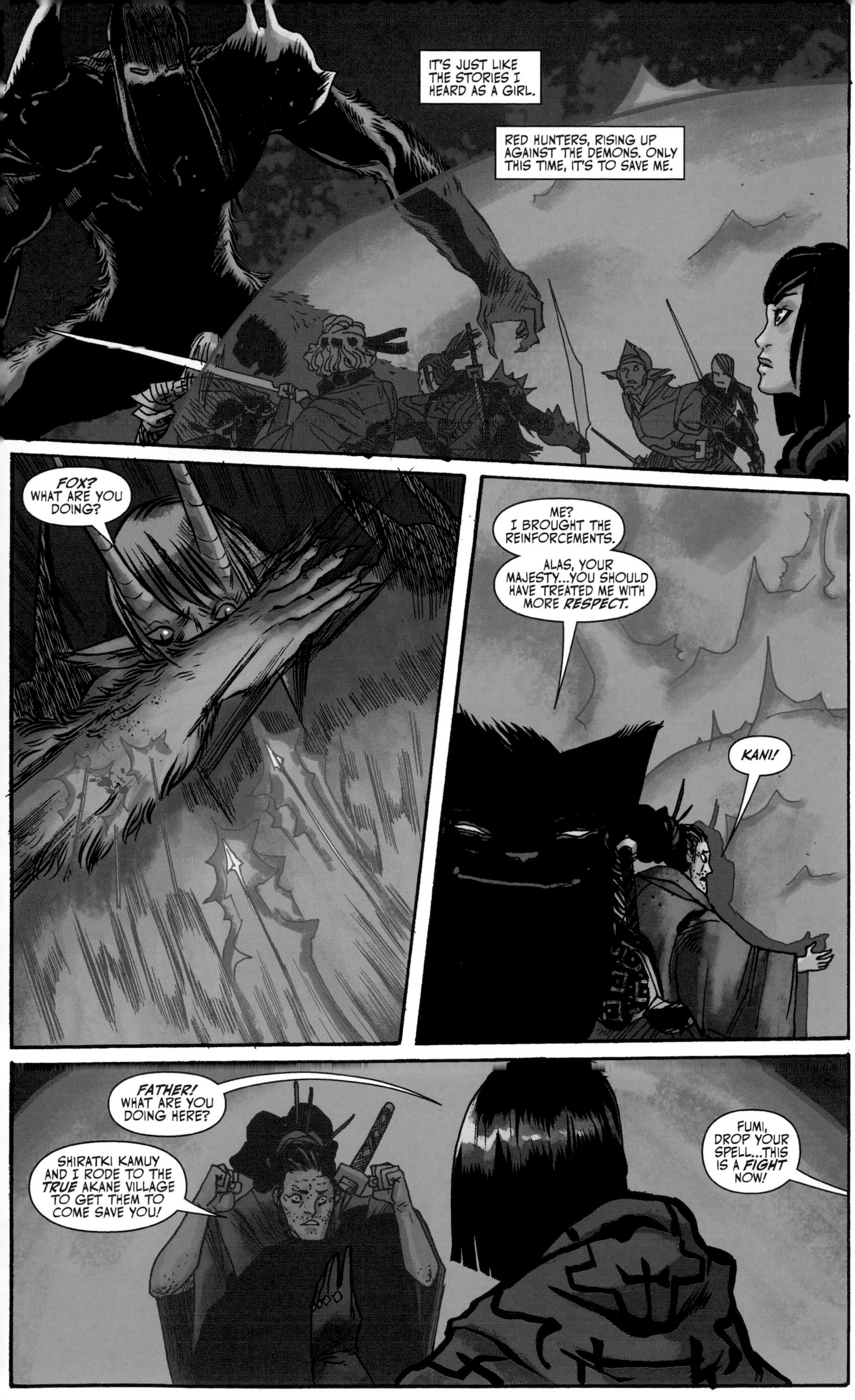
IT'S JUST LIKE THE STORIES I HEARD AS A GIRL.
RED HUNTERS, RISING UP AGAINST THE DEMONS. ONLY THIS TIME, IT'S TO SAVE ME.
FOX? WHAT ARE YOU DOING?
ME? I BROUGHT THE REINFORCEMENTS.
ALAS, YOUR MAJESTY...YOU SHOULD HAVE TREATED ME WITH MORE RESPECT.
KANI!
FATHER! WHAT ARE YOU DOING HERE?
SHIRATKI KAMUY AND I RODE TO THE TRUE AKANE VILLAGE TO GET THEM TO COME SAVE YOU!
FUMI, DROP YOUR SPELL...THIS IS A FIGHT NOW!

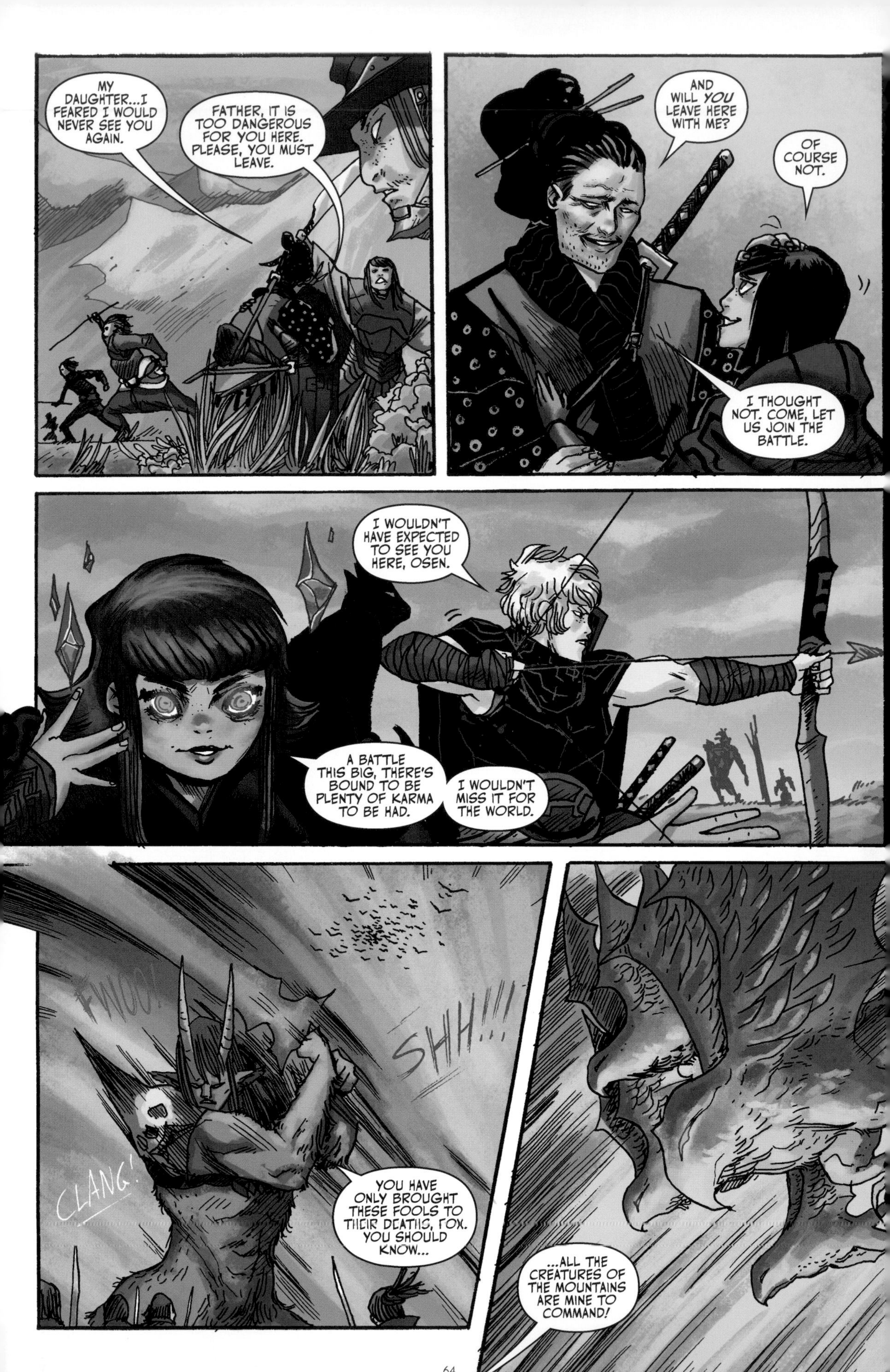
MY DAUGHTER...I FEARED I WOULD NEVER SEE YOU AGAIN.
FATHER, IT IS TOO DANGEROUS FOR YOU HERE. PLEASE, YOU MUST LEAVE.
AND WILL *YOU* LEAVE HERE WITH ME?
OF COURSE NOT.
I THOUGHT NOT. COME, LET US JOIN THE BATTLE.
I WOULDN'T HAVE EXPECTED TO SEE YOU HERE, OSEN.
A BATTLE THIS BIG, THERE'S BOUND TO BE PLENTY OF KARMA TO BE HAD.
I WOULDN'T MISS IT FOR THE WORLD.
FWOO!
SHH!!!
CLANG!
YOU HAVE ONLY BROUGHT THESE FOOLS TO THEIR DEATHS, FOX. YOU SHOULD KNOW...
...ALL THE CREATURES OF THE MOUNTAINS ARE MINE TO COMMAND!

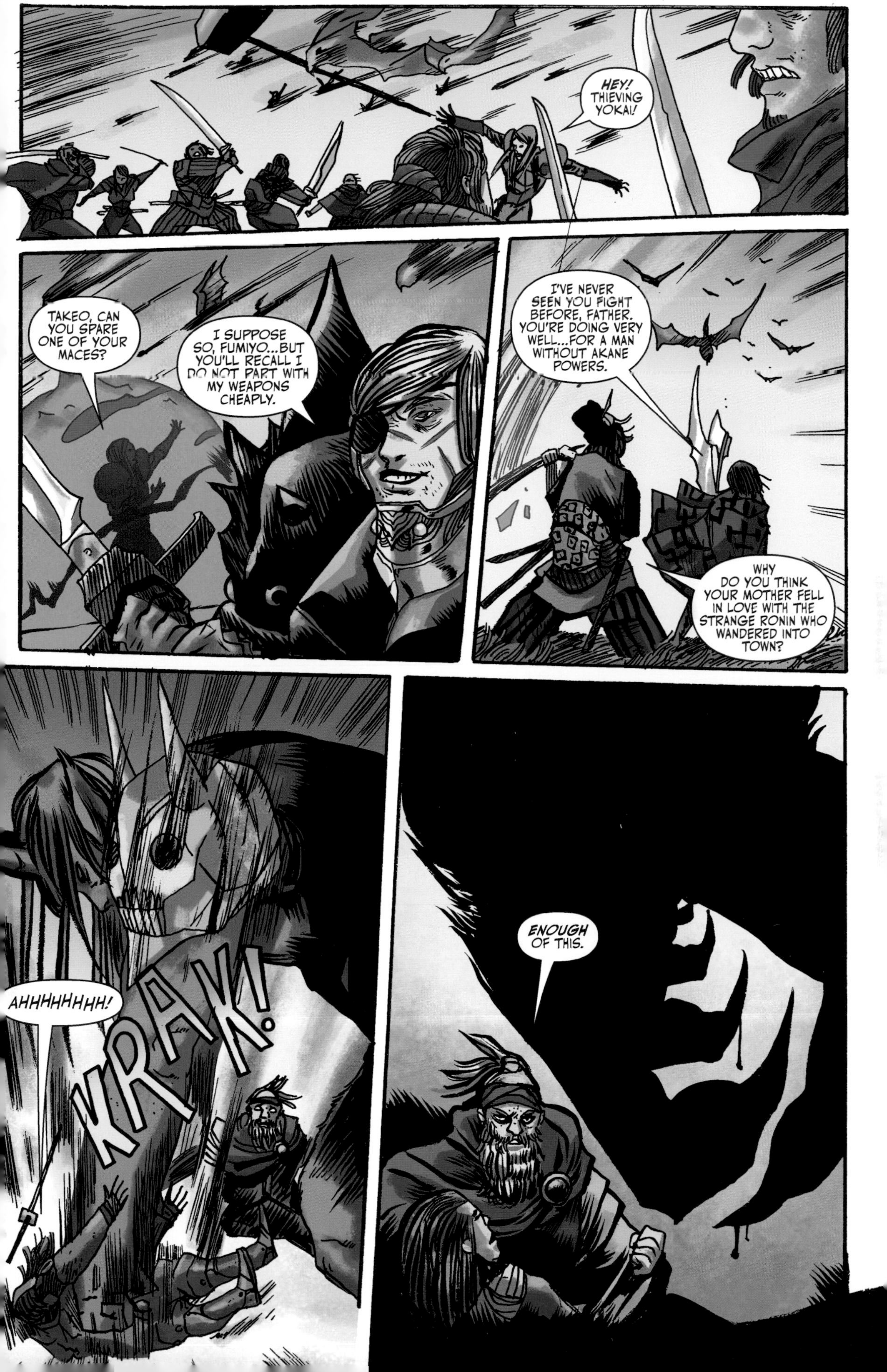
HEY! THIEVING YOKAI!
TAKEO, CAN YOU SPARE ONE OF YOUR MACES?
I SUPPOSE SO, FUMIYO...BUT YOU'LL RECALL I DO NOT PART WITH MY WEAPONS CHEAPLY.
I'VE NEVER SEEN YOU FIGHT BEFORE, FATHER. YOU'RE DOING VERY WELL...FOR A MAN WITHOUT AKANE POWERS.
WHY DO YOU THINK YOUR MOTHER FELL IN LOVE WITH THE STRANGE RONIN WHO WANDERED INTO TOWN?
AHHHHHHHH!
KRAK!
ENOUGH OF THIS.

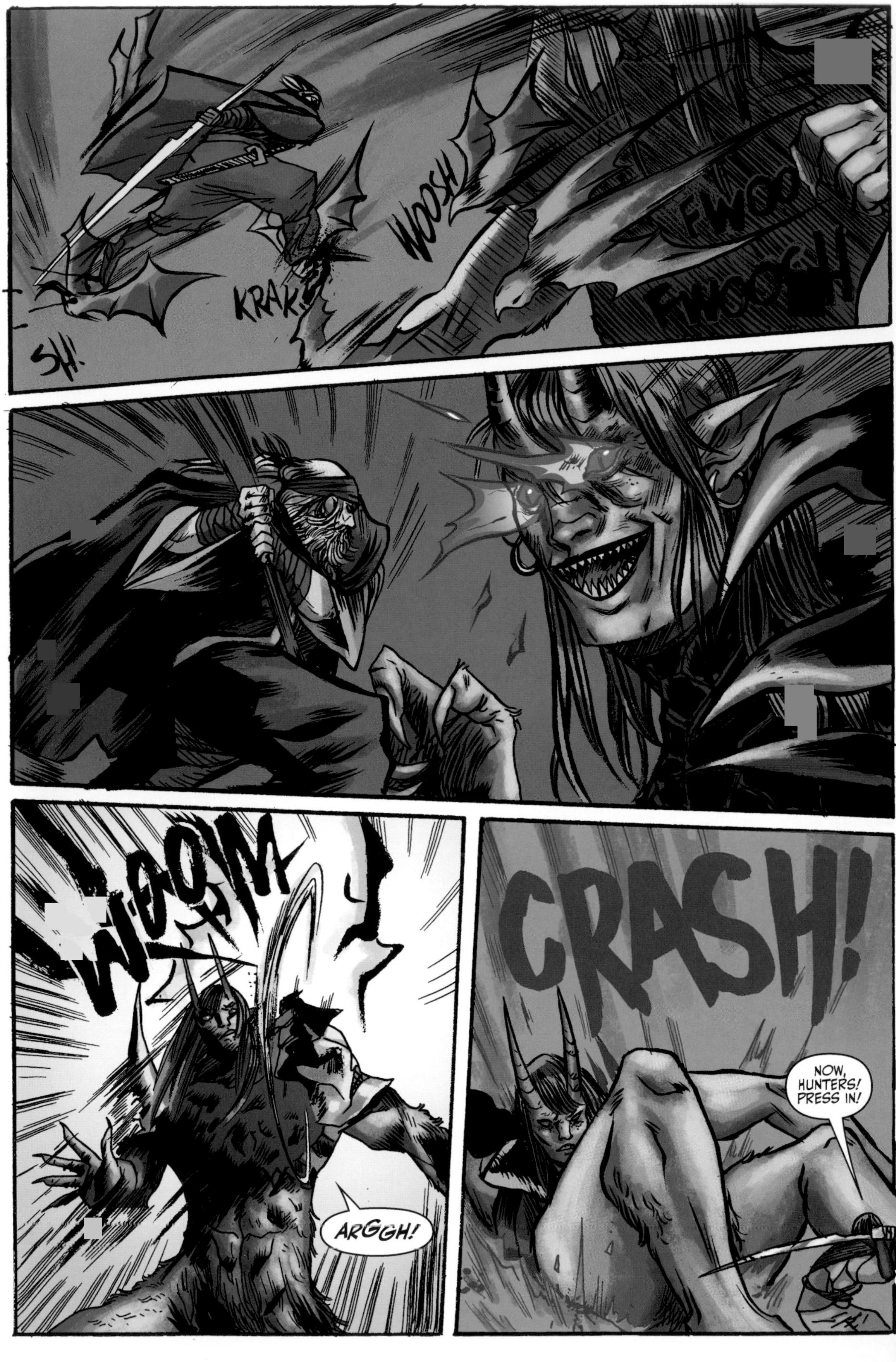
SH!
KRAK!
WOOSH
FWOOSH!
WOOM
ARGGH!
CRASH!
NOW, HUNTERS! PRESS IN!

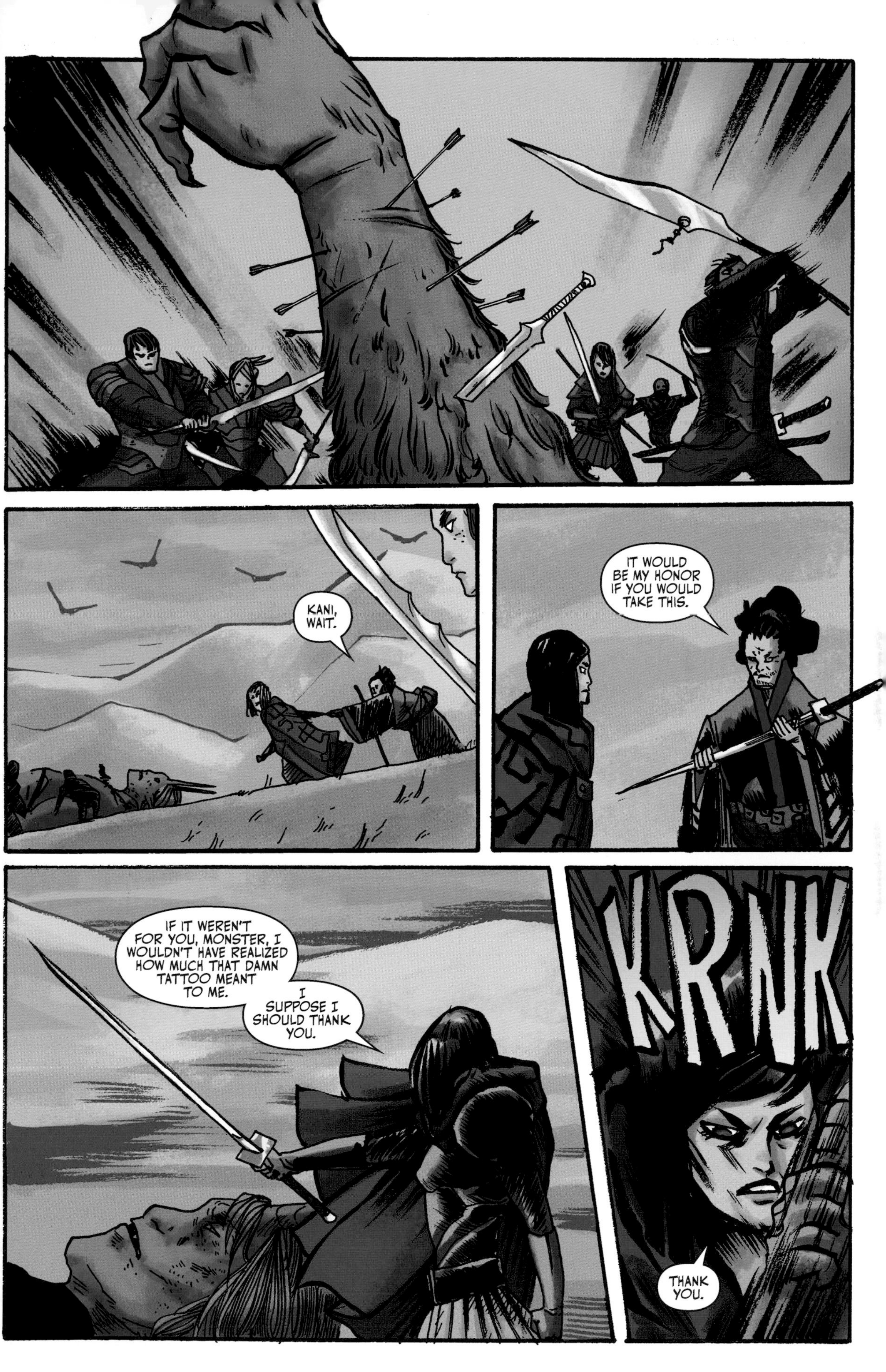
KANI, WAIT.
IT WOULD BE MY HONOR IF YOU WOULD TAKE THIS.
IF IT WEREN'T FOR YOU, MONSTER, I WOULDN'T HAVE REALIZED HOW MUCH THAT DAMN TATTOO MEANT TO ME.
I SUPPOSE I SHOULD THANK YOU.
KRNK
THANK YOU.

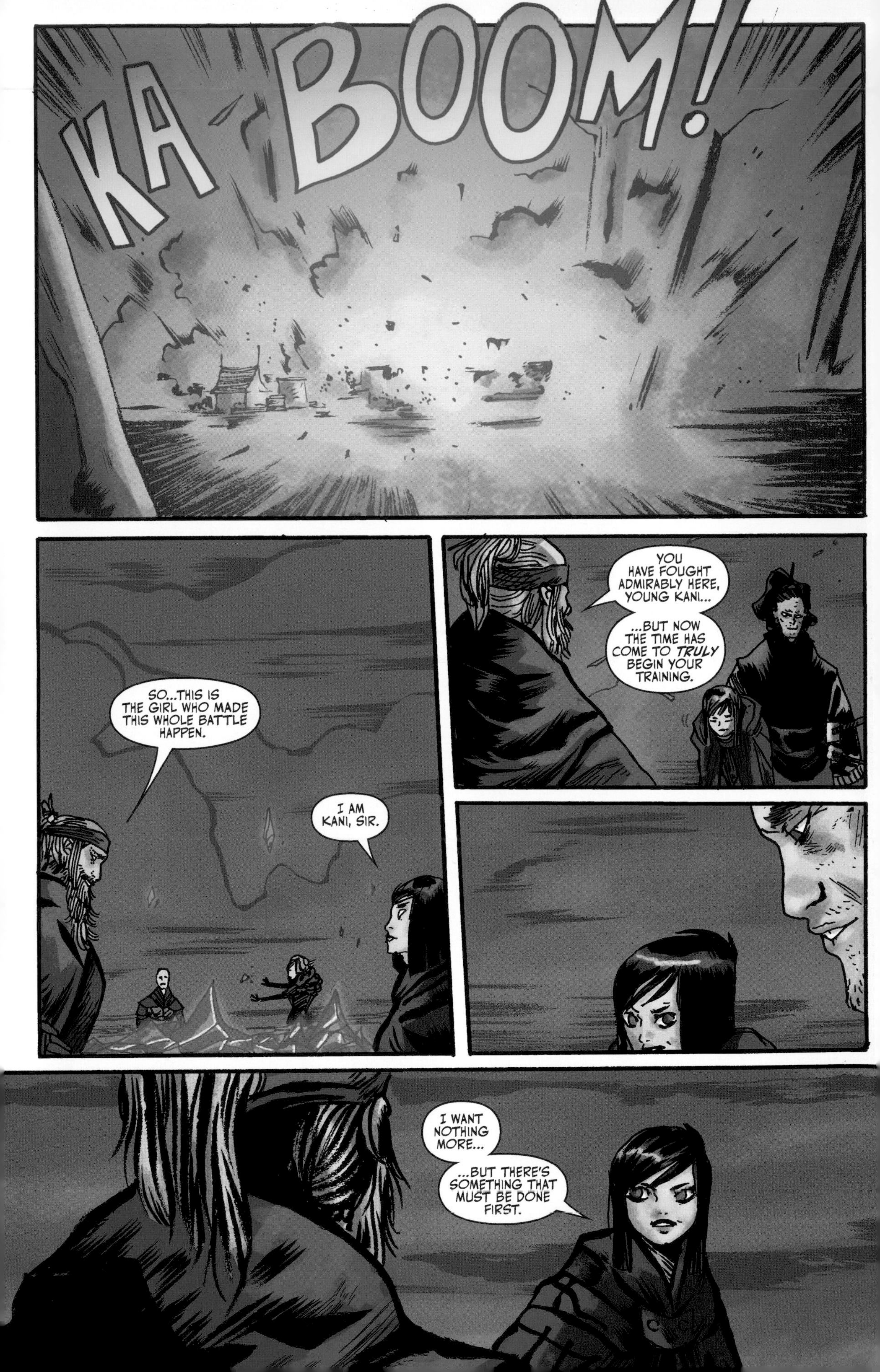
KA-BOOM!
SO...THIS IS THE GIRL WHO MADE THIS WHOLE BATTLE HAPPEN.
I AM KANI, SIR.
YOU HAVE FOUGHT ADMIRABLY HERE, YOUNG KANI...
...BUT NOW THE TIME HAS COME TO *TRULY* BEGIN YOUR TRAINING.
I WANT NOTHING MORE...
...BUT THERE'S SOMETHING THAT MUST BE DONE FIRST.

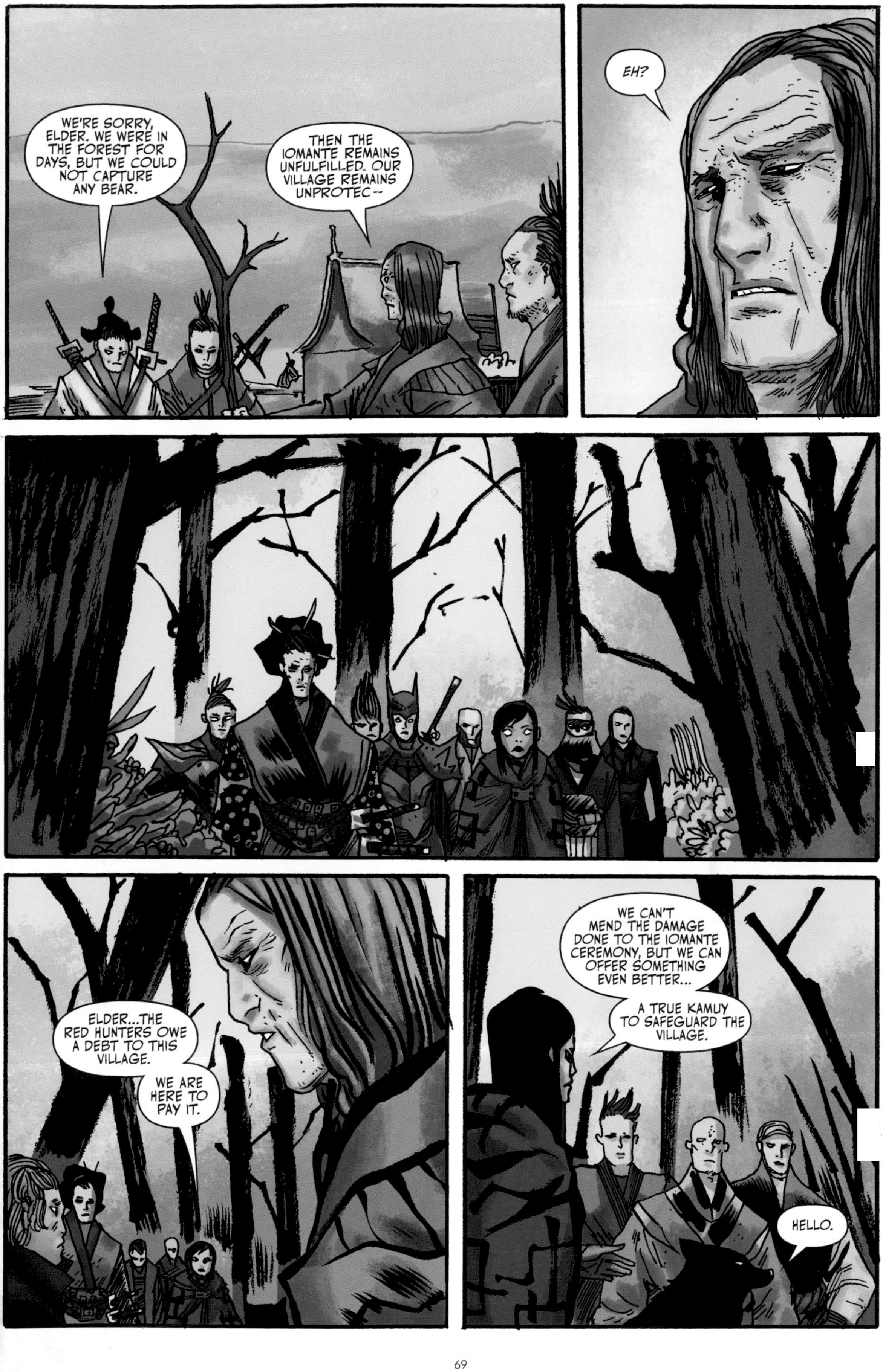
WE'RE SORRY, ELDER. WE WERE IN THE FOREST FOR DAYS, BUT WE COULD NOT CAPTURE ANY BEAR.
THEN THE IOMANTE REMAINS UNFULFILLED. OUR VILLAGE REMAINS UNPROTEC--
EH?
ELDER...THE RED HUNTERS OWE A DEBT TO THIS VILLAGE.
WE ARE HERE TO PAY IT.
WE CAN'T MEND THE DAMAGE DONE TO THE IOMANTE CEREMONY, BUT WE CAN OFFER SOMETHING EVEN BETTER...
A TRUE KAMUY TO SAFEGUARD THE VILLAGE.
HELLO.

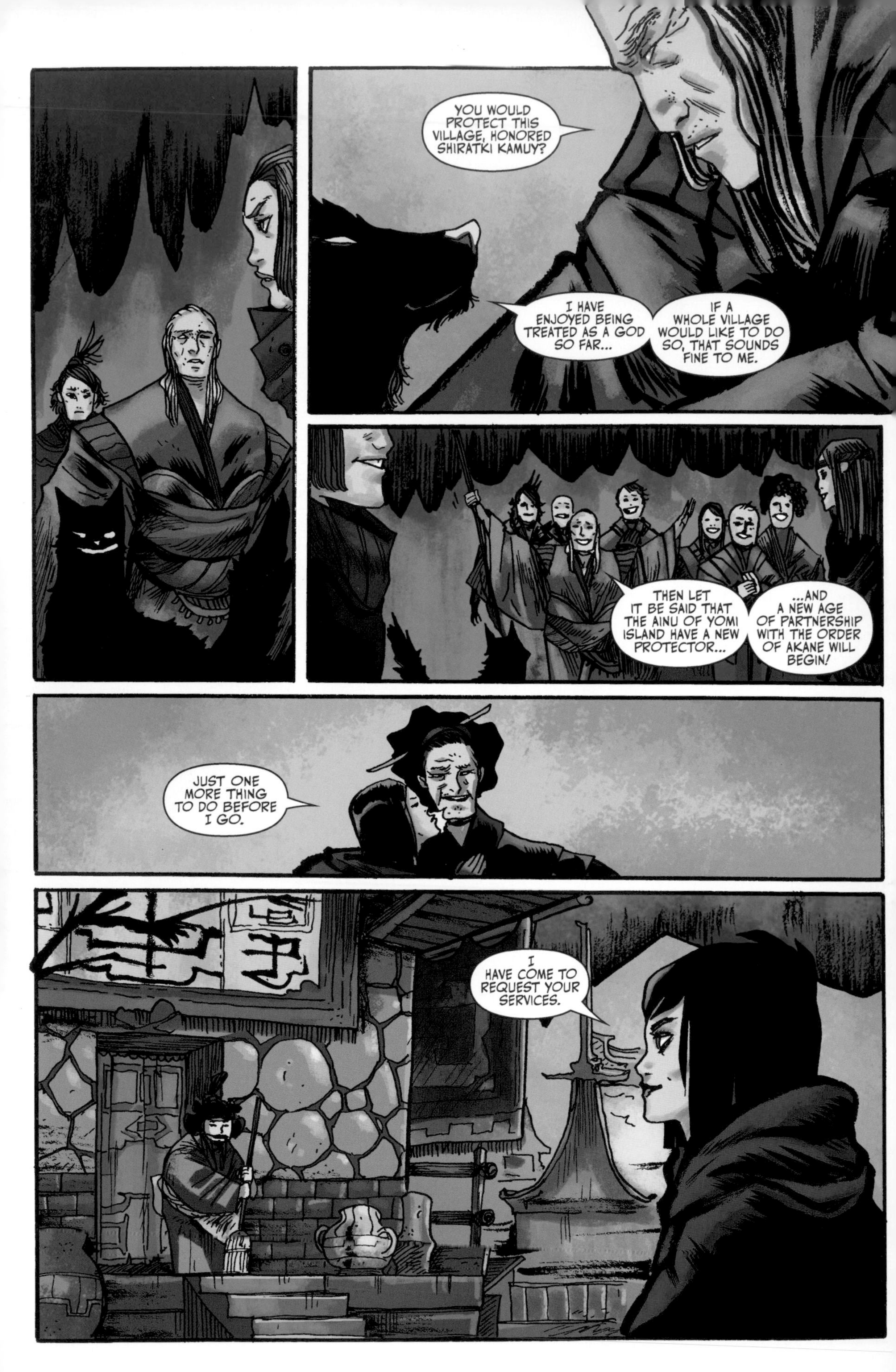
YOU WOULD PROTECT THIS VILLAGE, HONORED SHIRATKI KAMUY?
I HAVE ENJOYED BEING TREATED AS A GOD SO FAR...
IF A WHOLE VILLAGE WOULD LIKE TO DO SO, THAT SOUNDS FINE TO ME.
THEN LET IT BE SAID THAT THE AINU OF YOMI ISLAND HAVE A NEW PROTECTOR...
...AND A NEW AGE OF PARTNERSHIP WITH THE ORDER OF AKANE WILL BEGIN!
JUST ONE MORE THING TO DO BEFORE I GO.
I HAVE COME TO REQUEST YOUR SERVICES.

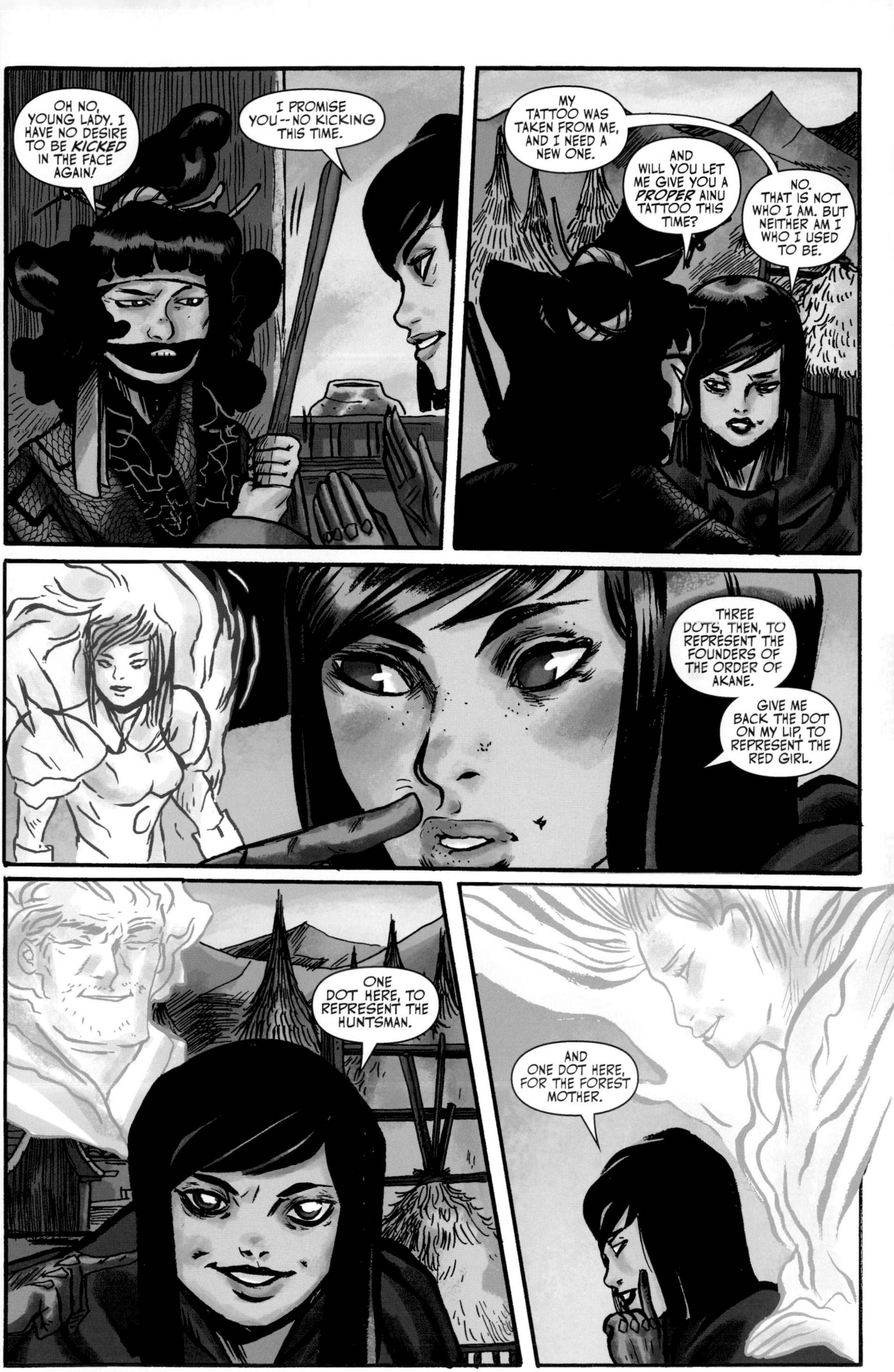
OH NO, YOUNG LADY. I HAVE NO DESIRE TO BE *KICKED* IN THE FACE AGAIN!
I PROMISE YOU--NO KICKING THIS TIME.
MY TATTOO WAS TAKEN FROM ME, AND I NEED A NEW ONE.
AND WILL YOU LET ME GIVE YOU A *PROPER* AINU TATTOO THIS TIME?
NO. THAT IS NOT WHO I AM. BUT NEITHER AM I WHO I USED TO BE.
THREE DOTS, THEN, TO REPRESENT THE FOUNDERS OF THE ORDER OF AKANE.
GIVE ME BACK THE DOT ON MY LIP, TO REPRESENT THE RED GIRL.
ONE DOT HERE, TO REPRESENT THE HUNTSMAN.
AND ONE DOT HERE, FOR THE FOREST MOTHER.

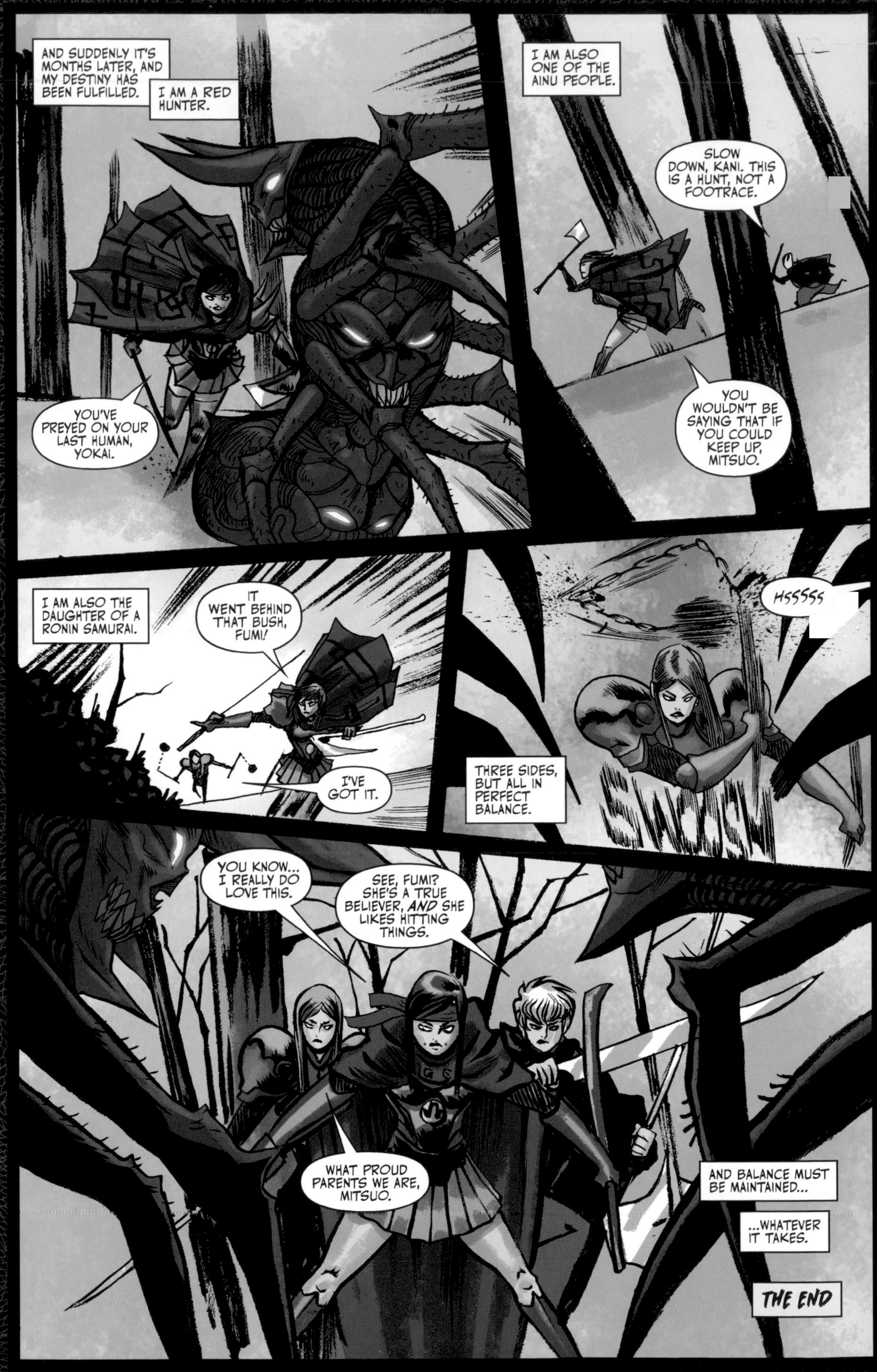

AND SUDDENLY IT'S MONTHS LATER, AND MY DESTINY HAS BEEN FULFILLED.
I AM A RED HUNTER.
YOU'VE PREYED ON YOUR LAST HUMAN, YOKAI.
I AM ALSO ONE OF THE AINU PEOPLE.
SLOW DOWN, KANI. THIS IS A HUNT, NOT A FOOTRACE.
YOU WOULDN'T BE SAYING THAT IF YOU COULD KEEP UP, MITSUO.
I AM ALSO THE DAUGHTER OF A RONIN SAMURAI.
IT WENT BEHIND THAT BUSH, FUMI!
I'VE GOT IT.
HSSSSS
THREE SIDES, BUT ALL IN PERFECT BALANCE.
SHOOSH
YOU KNOW... I REALLY DO LOVE THIS.
SEE, FUMI? SHE'S A TRUE BELIEVER, AND SHE LIKES HITTING THINGS.
WHAT PROUD PARENTS WE ARE, MITSUO.
AND BALANCE MUST BE MAINTAINED...
...WHATEVER IT TAKES.
THE END

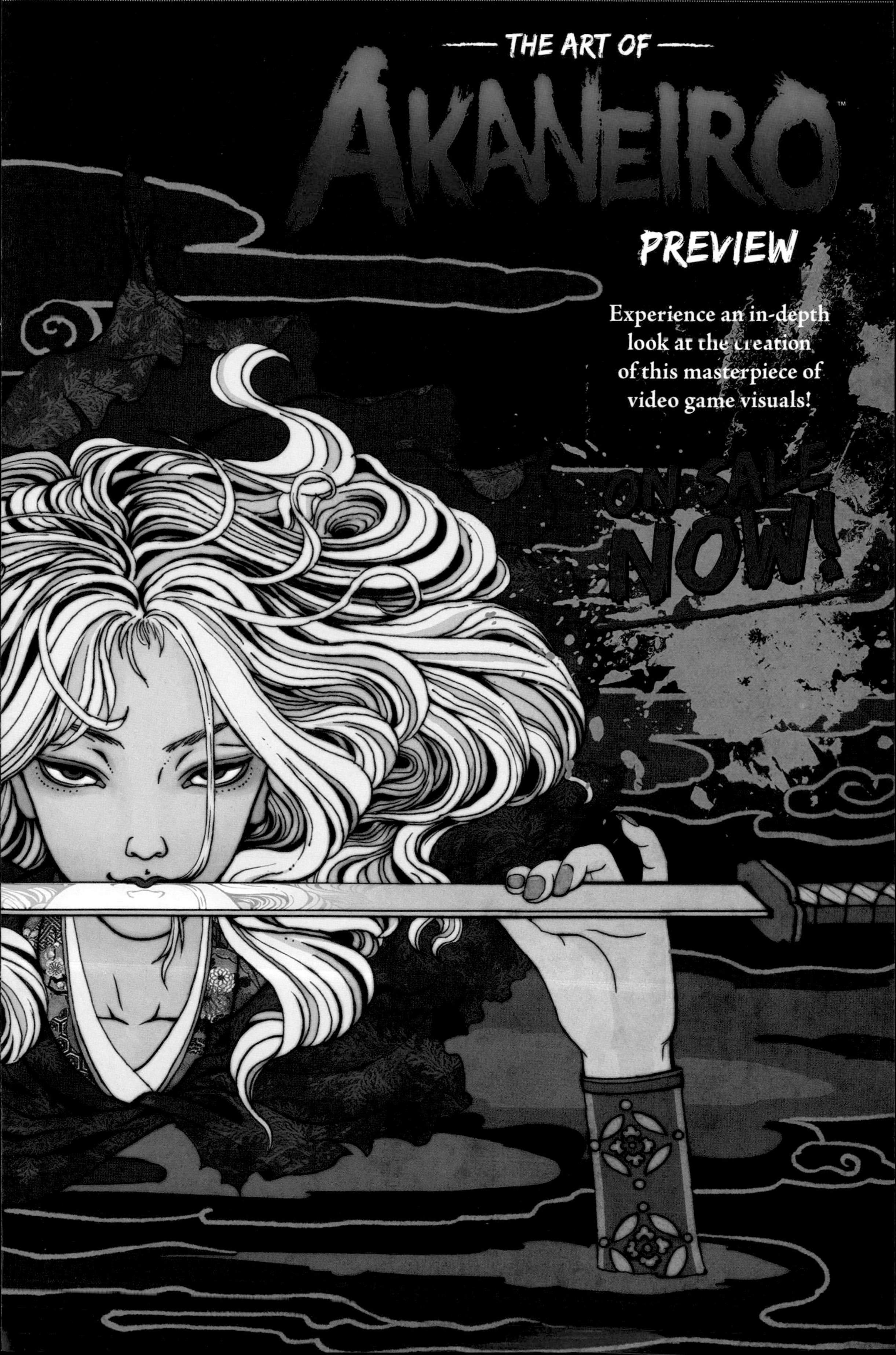
THE ART OF
AKANEIRO™
PREVIEW
Experience an in-depth look at the creation of this masterpiece of video game visuals!
ON SALE NOW!

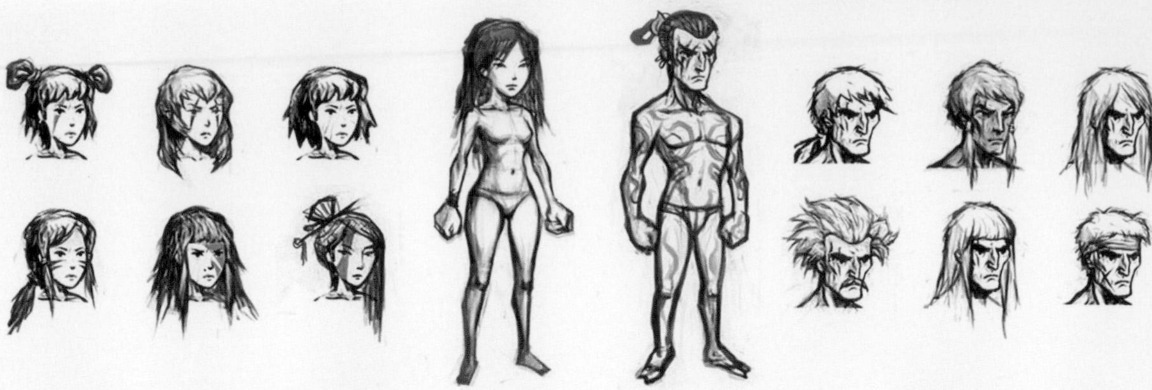

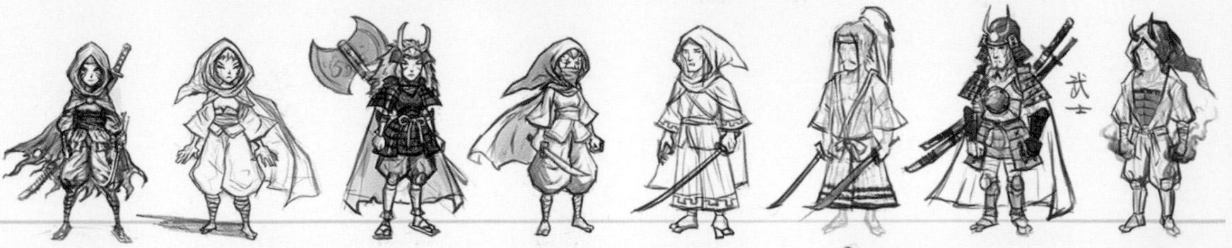

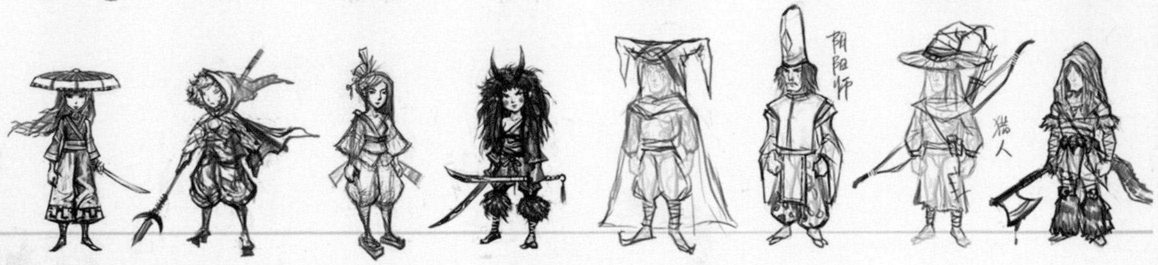

CHARACTER CLASSES

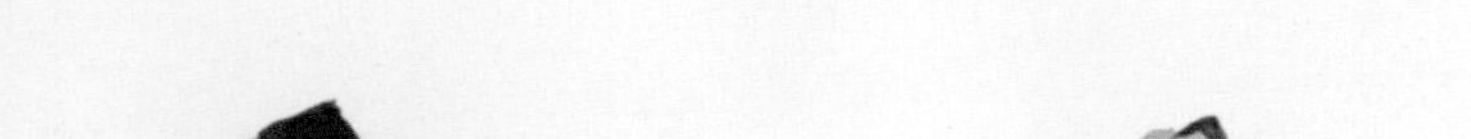

THIS SPREAD: The design for the Order of Akane evolved slowly. Initially, we drew and built a single character, Akaneiro, thinking everyone would play as her. But, for variety and flexibility, we decided to make the order an organization, so that players could take on any one of several characters. The art reflects our artists' sense of basic styling and costuming. They worked hard to craft several unique faces.

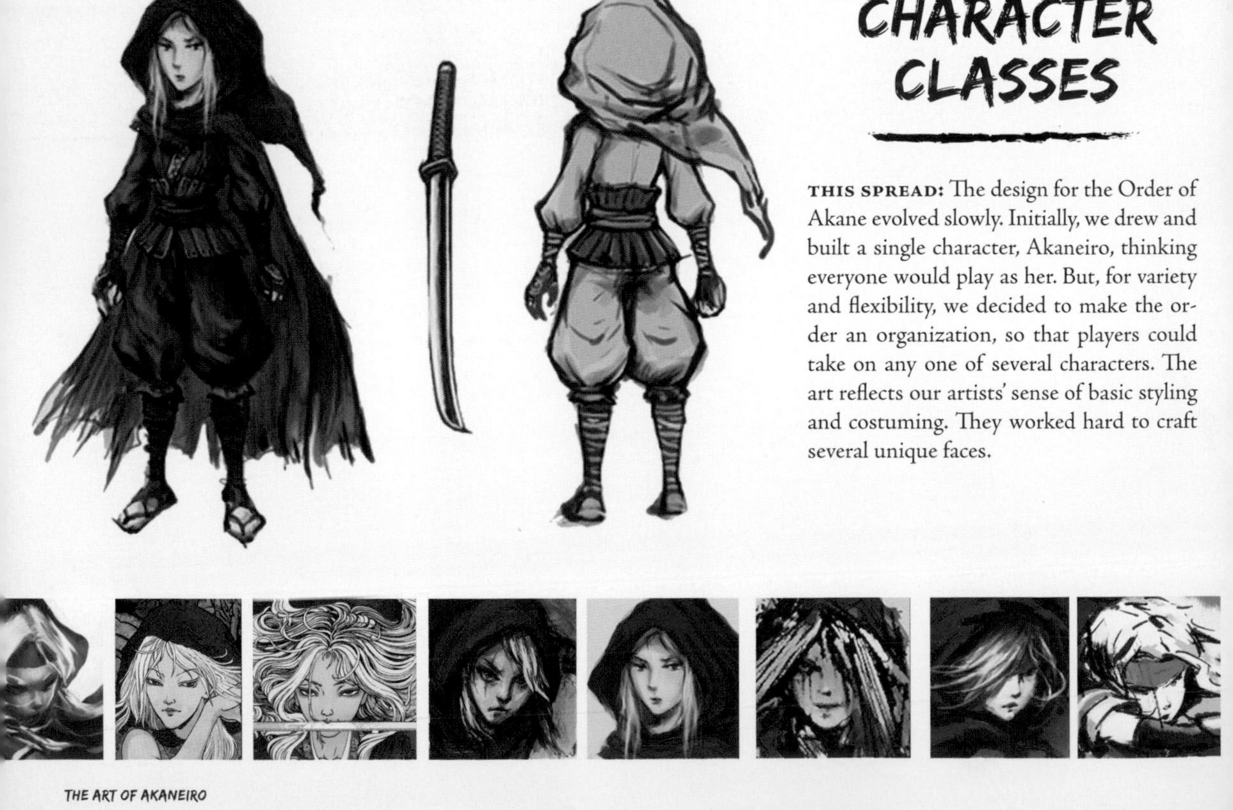

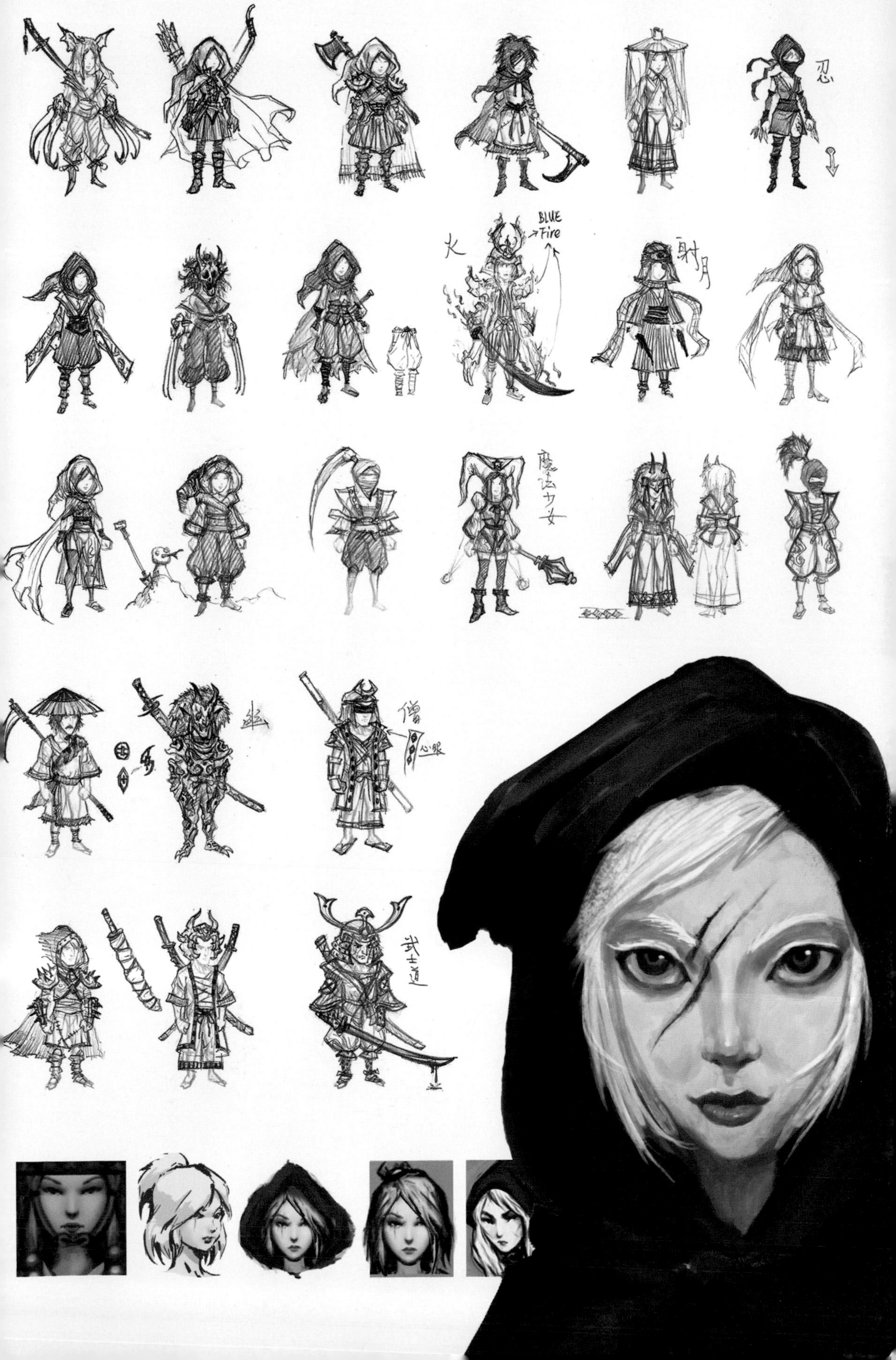
忍
BLUE
Fire
火
射月
魔法少女
僧
心眼
武士道

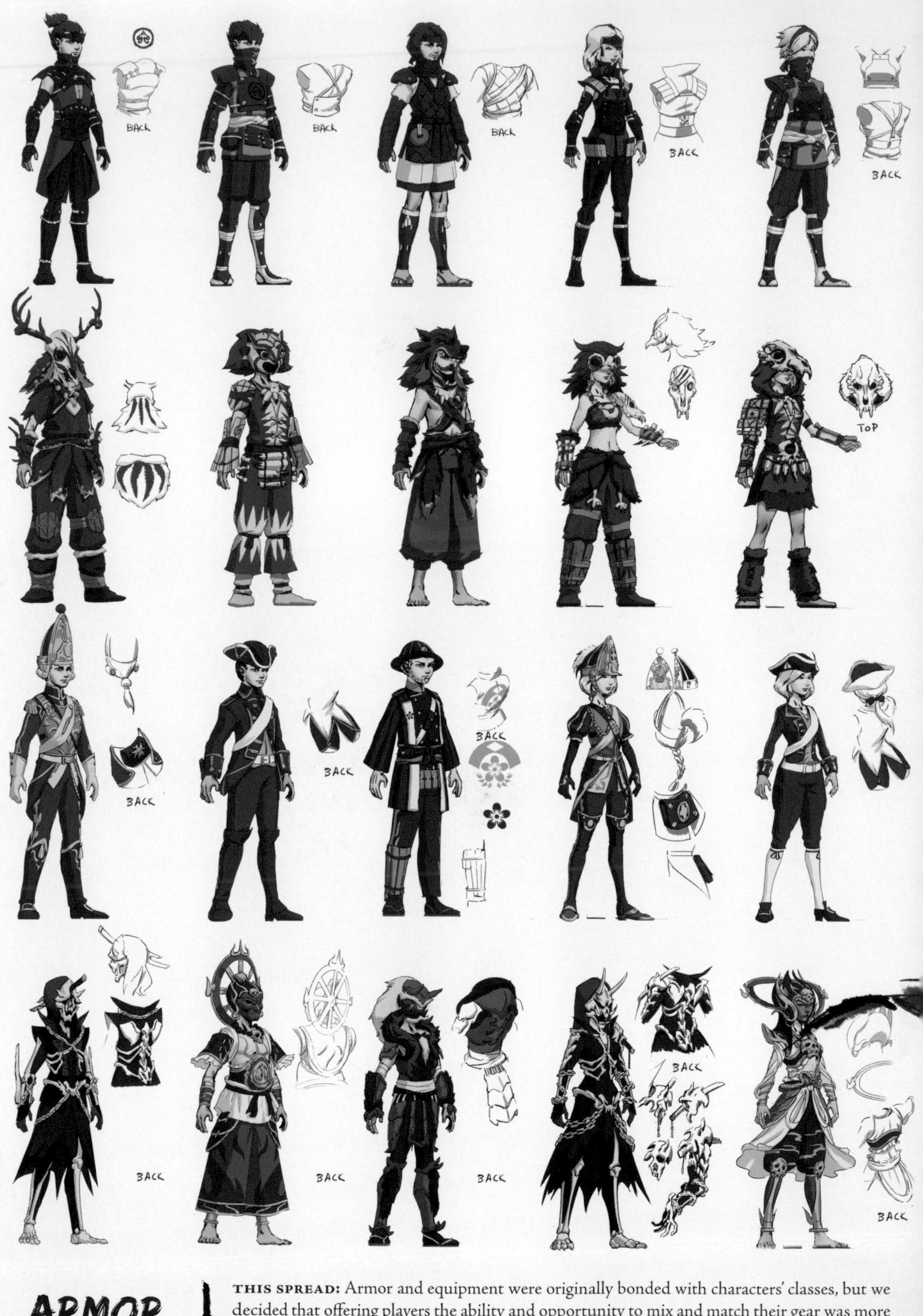
BACK
BACK
BACK
BACK
BACK
TOP
BACK
BACK
BACK
BACK
BACK
BACK
BACK
BACK
BACK
BACK

ARMOR CLASSES

THIS SPREAD: Armor and equipment were originally bonded with characters' classes, but we decided that offering players the ability and opportunity to mix and match their gear was more interesting and more fun.

Some of the crossover costumes produce surprising results. For example: when the Trapper set (representing the northern Ainu) and the Kabuki set (representing the southern Yamato) come together, it makes for a very cool combination.

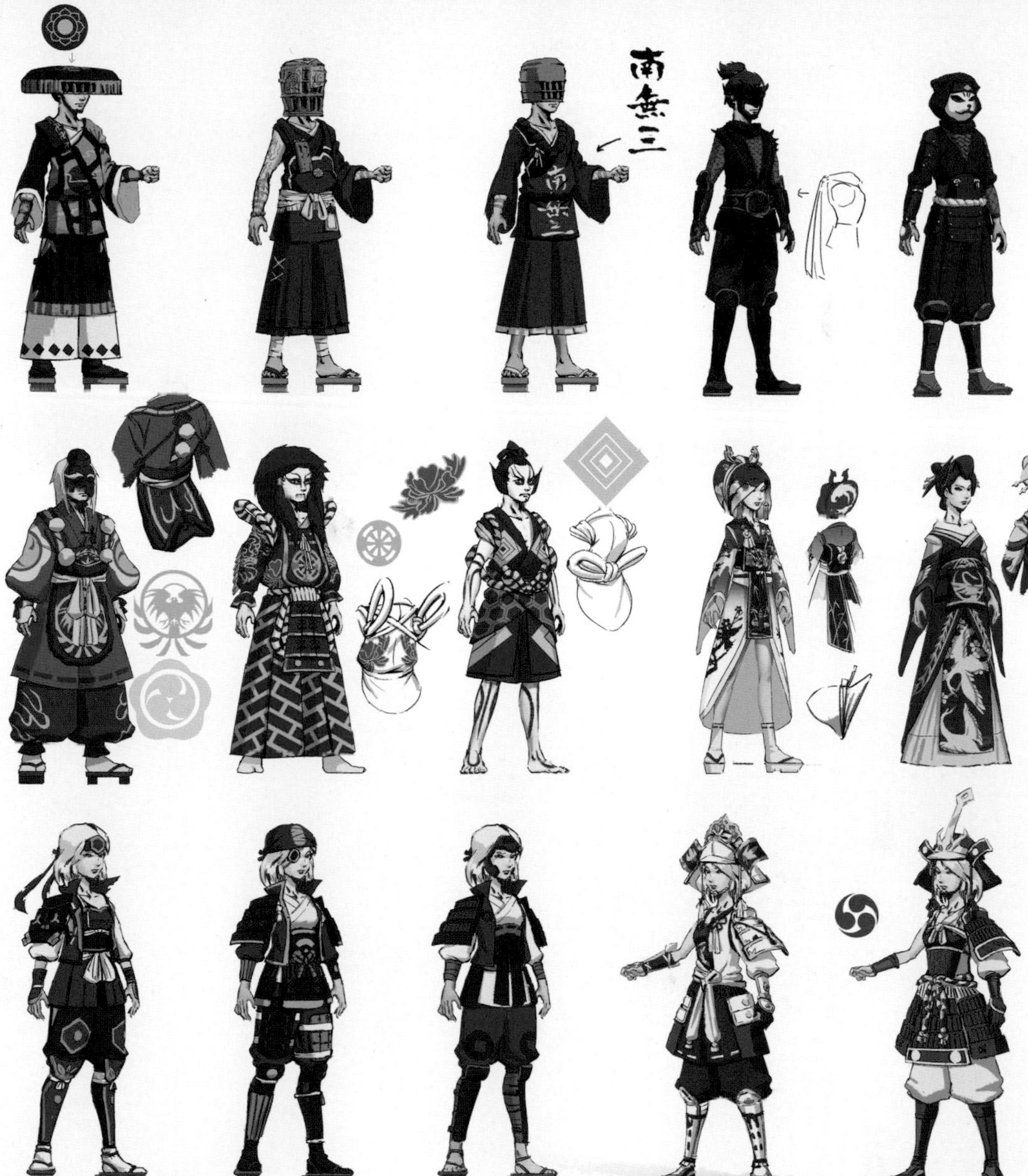
南無三

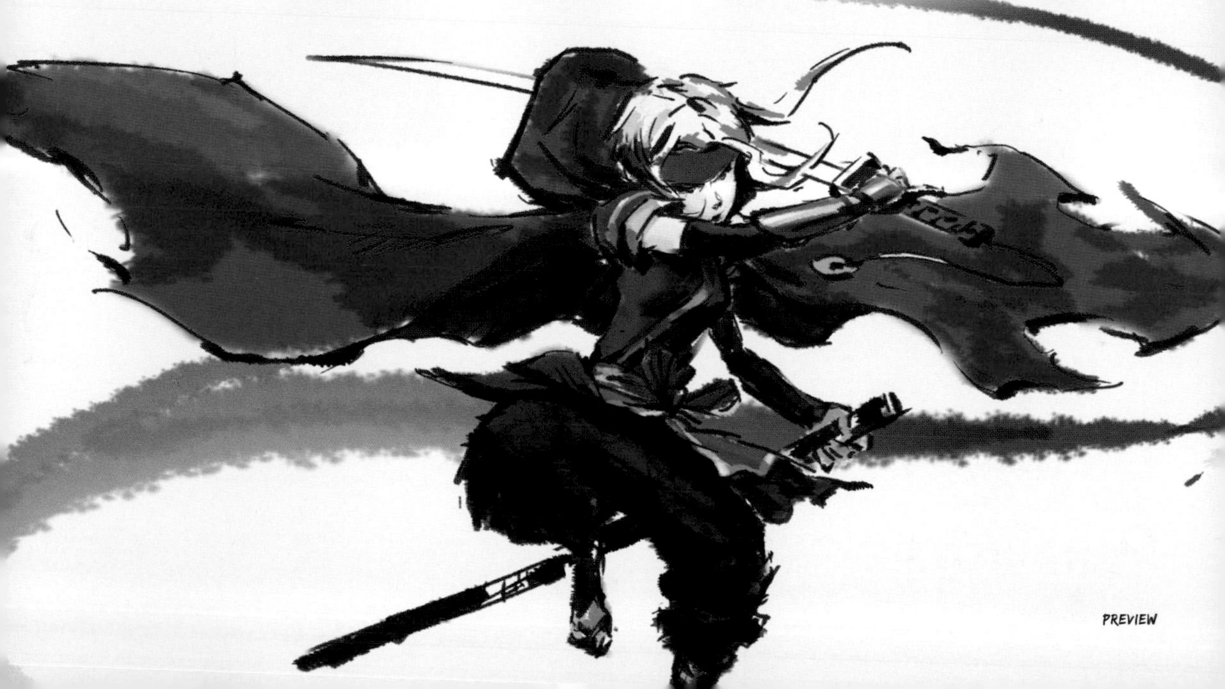

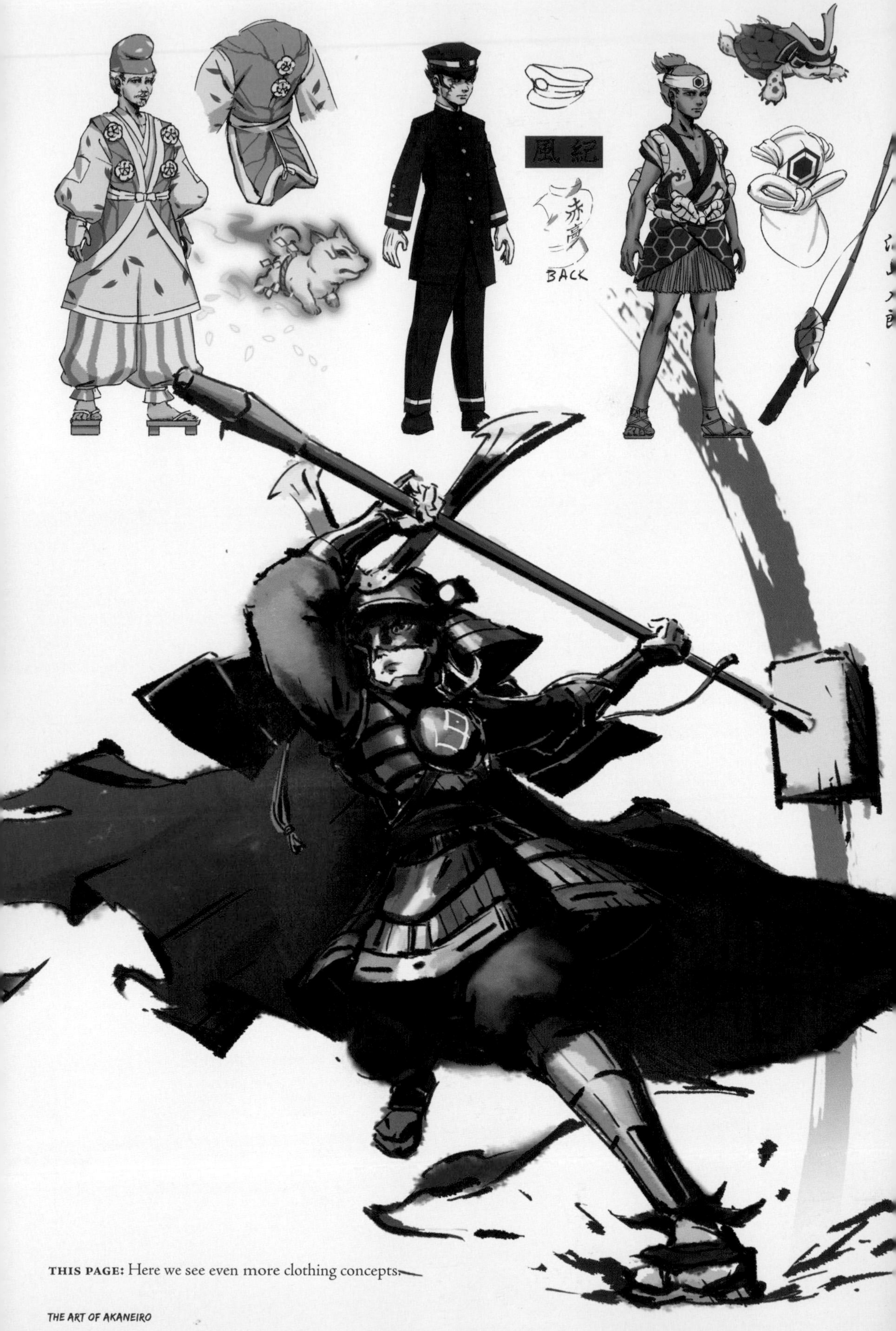
風紀
赤高
BACK

THIS PAGE: Here we see even more clothing concepts.

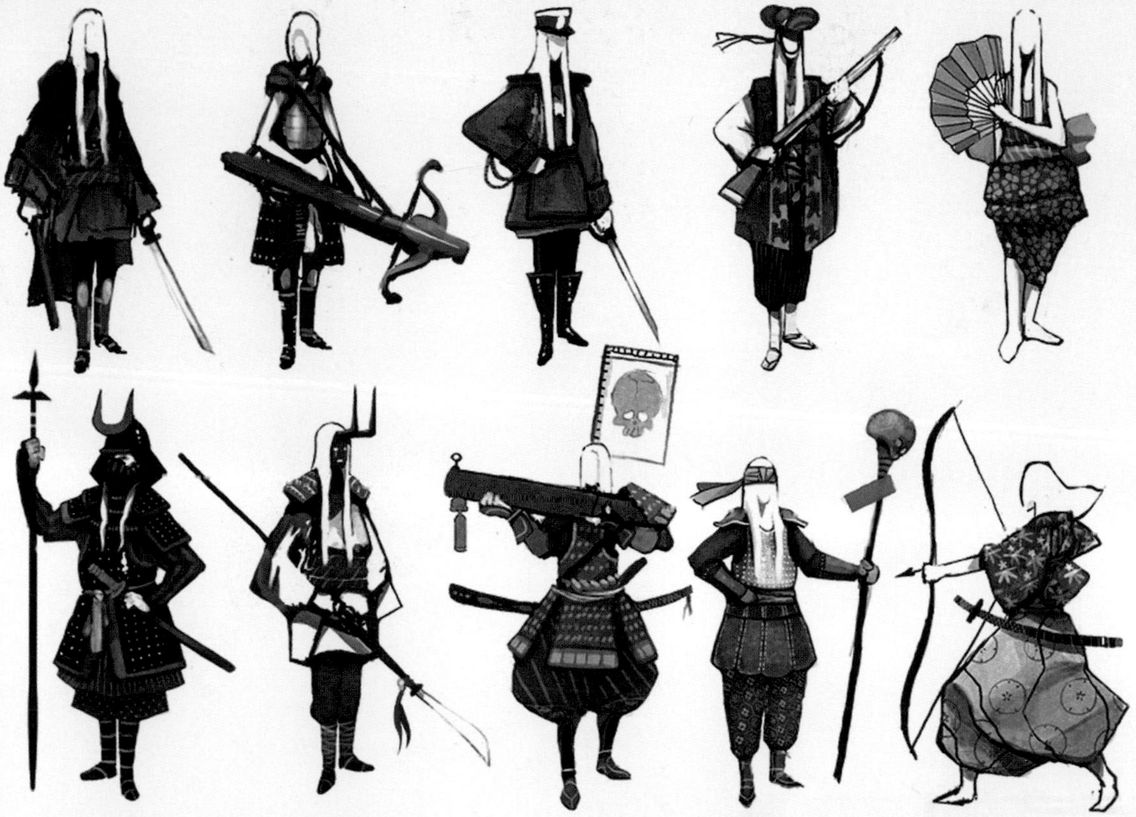

THIS PAGE: These silhouettes were created early on for selected costume designs. They allow for each costume to be immediately identifiable through a unique and distinctive shape.

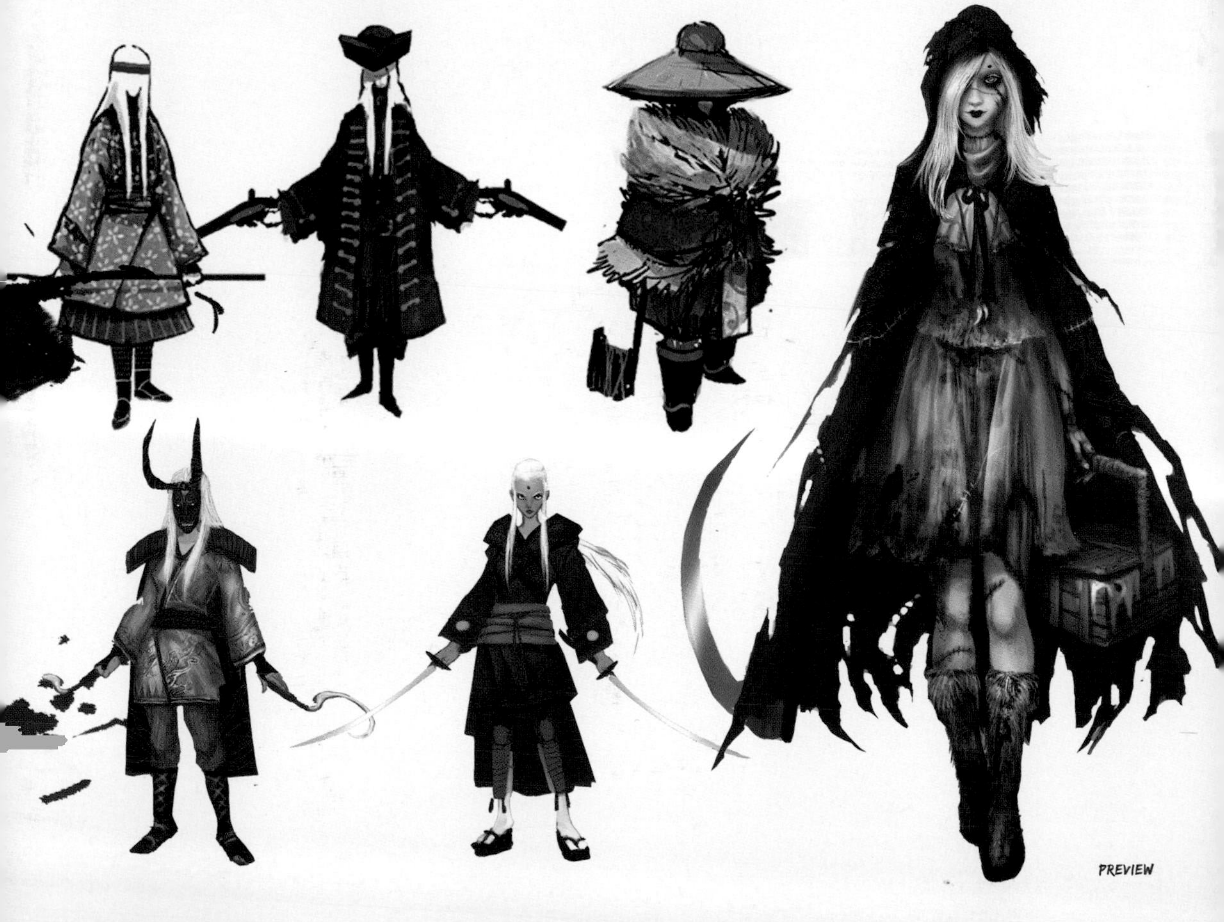